Essential System
Requirements

Addison-Wesley Information Technology Series

Capers Jones, Series Editor

The information technology (IT) industry is in the public eye now more than ever before because of a number of major issues in which software technology and national policies are closely related. As the use of software expands, there is a continuing need for business and software professionals to stay current with the state of the art in software methodologies and technologies. The goal of the Addison-Wesley Information Technology Series is to cover any and all topics that affect the IT community: These books illustrate and explore how information technology can be aligned with business practices to achieve business goals and support business imperatives. Addison-Wesley has created this innovative series to empower you with the benefits of the industry experts' experience.

For more information point your browser to
http://www.awl.com/cseng/series/it/

Wayne Applehans, Alden Globe, and Greg Laugero, *Managing Knowledge: A Practical Web-Based Approach.* ISBN: 0-201-43315-X

Gregory C. Dennis and James R. Rubin, *Mission-Critical Java™ Project Management: Business Strategies, Applications, and Development.* ISBN: 0-201-32573-X

Kevin Dick, *XML: A Manager's Guide.* ISBN: 0-201-43335-4

Jill Dyché, *e-Data: Turning Data into Information with Data Warehousing.* ISBN: 0-201-65780-5

Capers Jones, *The Year 2000 Software Problem: Quantifying the Costs and Assessing the Consequences.* ISBN: 0-201-30964-5

Ravi Kalakota and Marcia Robinson, *e-Business: Roadmap for Success.* ISBN: 0-201-60480-9

David Linthicum, *Enterprise Application Integration.* ISBN: 0-201-61583-5

Sergio Lozinsky, *Enterprise-Wide Software Solutions: Integration Strategies and Practices.* ISBN: 0-201-30971-8

Patrick O'Beirne, *Managing the Euro in Information Systems: Strategies for Successful Changeover.* ISBN: 0-201-60482-5

Bill Wiley, *Essential System Requirements: A Practical Guide to Event-Driven Methods.* ISBN: 0-201-61606-8

Essential System Requirements

A Practical Guide to Event-Driven Methods

Bill Wiley

Addison-Wesley

An imprint of Addison Wesley Longman, Inc.
Reading, Massachusetts • Harlow, England • Menlo Park,
California • Berkeley, California • Don Mills, Ontario •
Sydney • Bonn • Amsterdam • Tokyo • Mexico City

Many of the designations used by manufacturers and sellers to distinguish their products are claimed as trademarks. Where those designations appear in this book, and Addison Wesley Longman Inc. was aware of a trademark claim, the designations have been printed with initial capital letters or in all capitals.

This book contains material that has been extracted from the International Function Point Users Group (IFPUG) 4.1 Counting Practices Manual. It is reproduced in this book with the permission of IFPUG (http://www.ifpug.org).

The author and publisher have taken care in the preparation of this book, but make no expressed or implied warranty of any kind and assume no responsibility for errors or omissions. No liability is assumed for incidental or consequential damages in connection with or arising out of the use of the information or programs contained herein.

The publisher offers discounts on this book when ordered in quantity for special sales. For more information, please contact:

AWL Direct Sales
Addison Wesley Longman, Inc.
One Jacob Way
Reading, Massachusetts 01867
(781) 944-3700

Visit AW on the Web: www.awl.com/cseng/

Library of Congress Cataloging-in-Publication Data

Wiley, Bill, 1942–
    Essential system requirements: a practical guide to event-driven methods / Bill Wiley.
        p. cm. — (Addison-Wesley information technology series)
    Includes bibliographical references and index.
    ISBN 0-201-61606-8
    1. System design. 2. Management information systems. I. Title. II. Series.
QA76.9.S88 W53 1999
004.2′1—dc21   99–04584

ISBN 0-201-61606-8

Text printed on recycled paper

1 2 3 4 5 6 7 8 9 10—EB—0302010099

First printing, December 1999

In memory of Sandy—
a courageous lady who will never be forgotten
and without whom life will never be the same

Contents

PART I   Business Events and System Development

PART II Event-Partitioned System Requirements

PART III Estimating Software Projects

Preface

The Standish Group reports that tens of billions of dollars are wasted each year on information systems that are canceled or not used, with most projects over budget and/or late. On the other hand, the wrong system can be delivered on schedule, within budget. The primary problem has been that the system does not meet the expectations and needs of the business area for which it was built, typically because of inadequate user involvement in the early phases of system design. The challenge is to define the correct system requirements early in the delivery process to minimize design, construction, and post-implementation repair.

Accurate system requirements definition is a lost art for many organizations, but with the high cost of information systems and the competitive nature of business today, it is needed more than ever. An organization cannot afford to waste resources on post-requirements repair that could have been avoided. *Essential System Requirements* was written to provide a collection of event-driven methods for the analysis and specification of conceptual system requirements. I hope it will encourage and assist developers to "get it right the first time" by defining systems that are on target with the user's expectations. The term **essential**, as used in this book, refers to a set of system requirements that meets business-area needs without including unnecessary system capabilities. It also implies that the requirements are conceptual (non-physical) in nature. Although methods typically don't enforce a conceptual strategy, they can encourage the reduction of physical properties in the requirements. When this is accomplished, post-analysis repair can be reduced.

The most important aspect of this book is its underlying concept of business events and the partitioning of proposed systems into responses to those events. Business events are intuitive to the user and are typically accepted by both the user community and the development group. They get the user group involved early in the development life cycle by defining, in the user's language, activities that occur in the business area. Business events also help reduce the communication gap that often arises during the software development effort, and they partition the proposed system into subsystems that have relatively low coupling and support incremental development and implementation.

Essential System Requirements is a guide and therefore does not contain the amount of discussion found in most textbooks—discussion is limited to key basic concepts. It presents the methods and techniques in a concise manner to provide an effective instrument for the analyst, based on decades of software development experience. This book does not offer a particular commercial methodology but instead presents a set of core techniques and methods for the definition of system requirements. It follows a toolbox approach—that is, the methods and techniques are only used as needed, and are often repeated during the delivery process (some dependencies do exist, but iteration is the rule). For any particular project, some techniques may not be used at all. Along with the methods, this book integrates project management tips and a function-point project estimation method. It also offers a discussion of an object-oriented partitioning scheme that can be used with an event-driven user interface and that reuses many of the event-driven models.

Essential System Requirements will serve as a useful guide to the professionals responsible for the definition of system requirements and to those who manage the effort and develop the resulting system. As a guide, this book is meant to sit on your bookshelf, where, after initial study, it can be used for quick reference to the techniques and tips for the individual or the team. It can also support a corporate-wide effort to establish standards for the analysis and specification of system requirements.

For further discussion of the focus and organization of this book, please see the Introduction.

Acknowledgments

This book would never have been finished were it not for the initial encouragement from my wife Sandy, and although she never saw its completion, her memory was a continuous motivation.

I owe special thanks to my daughter Erin Bassett, who provided a critical eye and invaluable ideas as well as encouragement, and to my son Bruce, who offered technical advice and encouragement along the way.

To the students of the Information Systems Analysis and Information Systems Design classes at Taylor University, who continuously challenged me to find the answers and to stay on the leading edge, thank you all. And I thank my colleagues in the Computing and System Sciences Department at Taylor University for turning me loose with the analysis and design courses.

I thank my friend Jan Holm, with whom I had many valuable discussions during the early days of my search for a better way of building systems.

I am also grateful to my reviewers, each of whom contributed to the improvement of the original manuscript.

Finally, I thank my editor, Deborah Lafferty, who walked a first-time author through the process and stayed with the book when its outcome was doubtful. I would also like to thank my production coordinator, Tyrrell Albaugh, and others at Addison-Wesley who helped produce this book.

Introduction

An Executive Overview

Much of the business environment is being rethought and in many cases redesigned. Reduced time-to-market, improved customer service, and reduced costs are often critical factors in an organization's success and survival. Increasingly, Information Technology (IT) is expected to help firms meet their business challenges and must deliver new business-critical applications that are *on target*. With the dynamic nature of business today, a way must also be found to accelerate application development and to design and build adaptive systems.

One important factor in reducing the time it takes to develop information systems is to *get it right the first time*. The May issue of *Intelligent Enterprise*, states that about 75 percent of all software developed in the United States will never make it into production [1999]. The Standish Group [1995] reports that about $80 billion is wasted each year on information systems that are canceled or never used. A misconception that has been around for decades is that the sooner construction is begun, the sooner development will be completed. When requirements are not accurately defined and the subsequent system design is compromised, the cost of rework and the difficulty of maintenance more than offset whatever may have been gained by the reduced time-to-code. Another way to accelerate and focus the process is to use only those techniques that return value for any specific project. In the approach described in this guide, not every model component is required for every project.

This guide presents an approach that emphasizes accurate and complete requirements definition. It is also flexible and selective compared with past methodologies. This approach involves the user community very early in the development process, uses a strategy that is very natural to the business, and is adaptable to subsequent business change. Events jump-start the process of identifying and specifying requirements and therefore get the project off to a running start.

It is recommended that organizations adopt an accelerated, effective methodology for the system development process and require its use in all of their information system development projects. Also, well-run workshops between users and the requirements team (such as JAD) are powerful. They can shorten the requirements analysis and specification effort and, at the same time, increase quality. But they must be facilitated effectively and must have management's support throughout the organization. Management should insist on them. The remainder of this Introduction briefly discusses key topics of system development methods as well as the emphasis and organization of this book.

Contract Litigation Issues

More and more, organizations are turning to outsourcing for software, and, as a result, instances of litigation between these organizations and the contractors are increasing. Certainly, both the organization hiring outside resources and the contracted firm would like to avoid these conflicts. Jones reports that about 1 percent of software contracts end up in litigation. Other approximate outcomes between the parties of outsource agreements are shown below [Jones, 1999].

General satisfaction	70%
Some satisfaction	15%
Dissolution of agreement planned	10%
Litigation probable	4%
Litigation in progress	1%

One reason for contract conflict is that the development group has failed to produce a product that meets contract terms. There are several reasons why this can occur.

- A requirement that represents a needed response to a business event but not accurately

- A requirement that represents functionality that is not needed (a false requirement)

- Specifications that do not implement a true requirement accurately

- A deliverable that does not meet specifications

- Software that meets specifications but is poorly designed and is not easily maintained or enhanced

- Software that contains logic errors

There are additional causes of project and contract disagreements. Requirements can change because they were originally defined inaccurately and become better understood as the project progresses. Requirements can also expand because the users learn more about what the information system can do for them as the system is developed. Yet another problem is that a project is estimated inaccurately. These problems can manifest themselves in several ways.

- Schedule overruns

- Budget overruns

- Poor project resource allocation

- Software repair or additional development

Three activities, when done well, can reduce the risk of contractual issues and benefit both the buyer and the seller. Most of a project life cycle depends wholly or in part on the system requirements while both project size estimation and project management contribute significantly to project success.

System Requirements

Among all likely errors, poor system requirements pose the biggest liability risk to a contractor. Functions that are not needed can be built, and important functions can be missed. With failure to satisfy user expectations as the most dominant problem in software development today [Lewis, 1996], defining the system requirements is considered by many to be the most critical phase of the development life cycle.

Requirements form the foundation for all of the design, construction, and testing that follow; inaccuracies are reflected in later phases at a much greater repair cost. Since most of what happens downstream depends on the requirements, it is vital that a software development project have thorough, accurate requirements as a foundation. A missed or inaccurate requirement specification is difficult to detect during design, construction, and testing and is likely to escape detection until user acceptance testing.

Fixing the problem at a later point in the development cycle can cost more than 100 times the cost of repair that would have been incurred during the original requirements definition effort. These late repairs play havoc with project schedules and budgets; reduce the resources available for the new software development, since resources must now be used for software repair; and increase the project management load. On the other hand, good requirements allow for an "industry best" project estimate and focus the expenditure of resources on the design and development of the system represented by the complete set of true requirements.

An accurate system requirements package also reduces the risk of the requirements changing as the project progresses. Requirements "creep" is a major problem and averages about 2 percent per month for outsourced jobs [Jones, 1998]; many systems undergo much higher percentages of change. When requirements change, not only is completed work lost, but new tasks must be defined and scheduled and total system costs are impacted. When major changes occur, there can be a disruption of the development process that can be costly to both team productivity and team moral; this factor can be very difficult to measure.

But development teams must be able to detect and measure requirements change. Function points offer a way of defining an original baseline and then measuring and documenting the subsequent change so that the impact can be assessed and accurately represented to all parties of the contract.

One way to increase the chances of defining accurate requirements is to implement effective, modern methods across the organization. These methods should produce intuitive system partitions (such as business events), include an effective modeling strategy, and allow for user participation in the original analysis and specification effort as well as the subsequent verification of the requirements package.

Estimating Project Size

An equally important aspect of controlling schedule and cost overruns and effectively managing a project is the estimating process. Contractors can design and build applications very efficiently and accurately but still experience overruns and still be vulnerable to litigation because of poor estimating techniques. It is critical to the project management effort to have an accurate understanding of project size and content. But the complexity of the mix of project components makes each project unique, and historical data alone is not sufficient. Unfortunately, there is no totally dependable method of determining the magnitude of project effort.

The counting of application function points (Function Point Analysis, or FPA) is gaining popularity and is one currently available method that has an international user group that continually improves and refines the technique. Certification in FPA is also offered to allow an organization to take a serious approach to the estimating problem. Function points are counted on the basis of the system requirements and so are responsive to the variations of each individual application and don't depend on historical data alone for their estimation. Of course, this dependency on requirements places even more importance on accurate analysis and specification of those requirements. The combination of an event-driven system requirements definition methodology and function point analysis for project estimating can reduce the chances of contract litigation.

Project Management

Once an application has an accurate, comprehensive set of requirements and an accurate estimate of project size, the next thing that has to happen is effective project management. Project management is composed of the following components.

- Planning

- Scheduling

- Monitoring

- Controlling

- Directing

All of the five activities listed above are affected in some way by the requirements. Many of the project tasks are based on the system partitions that are established by the strategy used for the requirements definition; in this book, that strategy is event based. Project management applies the five components to the design, construction, testing, and implementation of each of the event responses. This in effect is like managing the development of many relatively small subsystems and provides the following advantages.

- Each event response has high cohesion and low coupling.

- Each event response can be assigned to a team and taken vertically through the life cycle while another team is investigating new business events.

- Teams can be narrowly focused on a single event and work autonomously.

- Progress and task completion can be controlled more easily because of the autonomous nature and relatively small size of each event response.

- Each event response is persistent throughout the life cycle and can be identified in the design, construction, and testing phases and as well as during and after implementation.

- With intuitive system partitions, all participants (users, management, and developers) have a clearer view of the project tasks.

The event-partitioning scheme provides an intuitive way of identifying each system partition that facilitates communication between teams, between management and developers, and between users and developers. It also accommodates a response to changing requirements. Since business events have their origins in the user domain, event responses are tightly focused on the response to a business event and it is easier to isolate changes to a partition of specifications or a partition of code. This facilitates assessment of the impact and the subsequent implementation of the change.

Summary

The combination of an event-driven system requirements definition methodology, function point analysis for project estimating, and a project management strategy based on business events gives an organization a reasonable chance to develop an application that is on target and on schedule.

Capers Jones describes seven ways to minimize the risk of contract conflict and subsequent litigation [1999].

1. The sizes of software contract deliverables must be determined during negotiations, preferably using function points.
2. Cost and schedule estimation must be formal and complete.
3. Creeping user requirements must be dealt with in the contract in a way that is satisfactory to both parties.

4. Some form of independent assessment of terms and progress should be included.
5. Anticipated quality levels should be included in the contract.
6. Effective software quality control steps must be utilized by the vendor.
7. If the contract requires that productivity and quality improvements be based on an initial baseline, then great care must be utilized in creating a baseline that is accurate and fair to both parties.

For contractors and clients alike, these guidelines can reduce the chances of ending up in litigation.

Modern System Development Methods with Events

A modern methodology is a toolkit of techniques and guidelines for building reliable, resilient software. Formal system development methodologies have been around since the 1970s and the debate about their value versus the time spent has been around for about as long. With the dynamic nature of business today and the resulting need for shorter delivery cycles, the older methodologies are just too slow.

Since an information system models some part of the business, it must be responsive to change. This implies shorter delivery periods so that proposed systems will undergo less change during the development life cycle. It also implies methods that allow requirements adjustment in response to a business change and to a better understanding of the business under study. Iterative, spiral approaches that deliver increments of a system address part of the resiliency issue. A software structure that is easily maintained is another important part. The following discussion will examine event-driven methods and how they relate to some of the current popular development approaches.

Life Cycle/Delivery Process

Every software development project has an underlying life cycle. First determine what is required, next design a physical solution, and finally build and implement the solution. But the delivery process used for a system does not have to follow the life cycle in a stepwise fashion. Paul Allen and Stuart Frost [1998] present an iterative delivery process that includes prototyping and can divide the project into increments that are more responsive to business needs (see Figure I.1). This

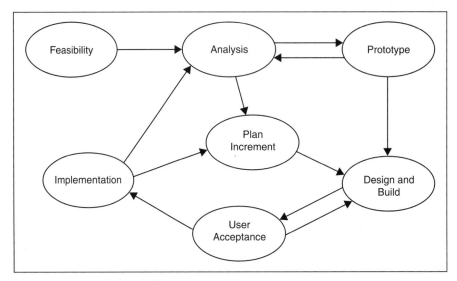

Figure I.1   Iterative delivery process

delivery process works well with an event-driven, event-partitioned approach and will be followed in this book.

Profile of a Business Event

The definitions of "business event" and "event response" used in this book are taken from *Essential Systems Analysis* by Stephen McMenamin and John Palmer: "An *event* is some change in the system's environment, and a *response* is the set of actions performed by the system whenever a certain event occurs" [1984]. An event response lies idle until receipt of the trigger, at which time it completes all processing and then returns to an idle state to await another instance of the trigger. "When a system's response to an event has been determined before the event occurs, then the interactive system generates a *planned response.* . . . Planned response systems don't react to every event in the environment. Many external and temporal events don't even raise a yawn from a particular system" [McMenamin and Palmer, 1984]. In some cases, depending on the context in which *event* is used, this book will add "business" to the term to distinguish it from a screen event that is common to a language such as Visual Basic. It will also use the term "event response" rather than just "response."

Two of the more compelling properties of an event-driven methodology are the natural partitions that are established in the user interface and the subsequent partitions of the information system that persist throughout the design and implementation phases. These partitions are highly independent subsystems (have very low coupling) that interface only with the users and stored data. They promote involvement by the user since they are described in the user's language and since they describe the user's work activities. They also continue to be recognizable throughout the development process, facilitating communication between the development team and the user group. This persistence also aids traceability from code back to requirements.

But how does an event-partitioned approach match up with the popular approaches of spiral, incremental, Rapid Application Development (RAD), and "proof of concept" prototyping? This question will be examined in the next few subsections.

Partitioning Schemes

The requirements definition process defines the user interface with the identification of business events that occur outside the system boundary. When an *event-partitioning* scheme is chosen for the system partitioning (inside the system boundary), a response to each business event is defined by its user interface, its processing requirements, and its interface to stored data and is encapsulated in a single conceptual unit. In effect, the event-driven user interface is extended to include the partitioning of the entire system. However, when an *object-partitioned* approach is used, the system is partitioned by object classes. The response to a business event is not encapsulated into a single processing unit but is spread across object classes as methods (or services). These two approaches are represented in Figure I.2.

For every business event occurring outside the system, event partitioning defines a partition of the system dedicated to responding to the business event. When the system is partitioned around object classes, there can be a number of classes required to respond to a business event. In each case, the system is treated as a black box that responds to business events that occur in the environment. Each event response is triggered by a single input from outside the system and will result in changes in the stored data and/or outputs to external agents in the system's environment. The difference occurs in how an event response is organized.

Data Model

Thorough, conceptual data modeling early in the delivery process accomplishes a number of things. First, there are more business rules documented in the data

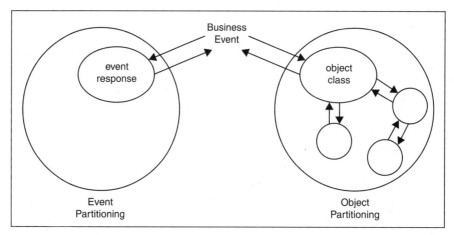

Figure I.2   Partitioning schemes

model than in any of the process models. Development of a complete, normalized data model is not possible without knowledge of the business of the proposed system. Also, the relationships in an Entity Relationship Diagram (ERD) have a close link to the system's business events. This provides a valuable cross-check between the ERD and the system business event list.

Another vital role of early data modeling is to provide the opportunity to test the data as the process models are developed. If the data model does not support the processing, it is much better to find it during requirements definition rather than later when it has much more impact.

Identifying attributes early forces a detailed understanding of the requirements while the development team has close contact with the user group (hopefully using joint sessions such as JAD) and response to change is less expensive.

A data model is very valuable to the requirements effort when developed early in the delivery process since it is rich in business rules, must support the processing of the proposed system, and can be tested in the form of a model.

Spiral or Waterfall

The *waterfall approach* suggests that each phase be completed in its entirety before considering subsequent phases without plans or the option to return to earlier, completed phases. The problem with the waterfall approach is that it proceeds as if the business and thus the system under study will not change during development. Many organizations that use a waterfall approach demand a sign-off by the user to freeze the requirements so that changes will not have to be considered until the system is in maintenance. Of course, by the time it is implemented, the system no longer models the business and in many cases is unusable.

The *spiral approach* to systems development is accomplished by iterating through the delivery process with a little analysis, a little design, a little build and test, and back to more analysis. This takes advantage of the learning that occurs as the development team moves through the delivery process and provides the opportunity to apply the new understanding, along with changes that occur in the business, before implementation.

With the low coupling between partitions, each event response can be developed as a separate, independent subsystem. This low coupling of the event responses provides flexibility in the iteration between the delivery process stages. All the while the data model is tested and modified as needed.

A spiral approach supports *incremental development* as the independent nature of each event response allows for both vertical and horizontal development to proceed in parallel. That is, one or more event responses can be developed vertically through the design, build, and implementation phases while the conceptual definition of other event-response requirements is taking place. Since a conceptual understanding of the input and output needs of each event response is documented in the requirements phase, the data dependencies between the event responses can be examined and delivery increments planned.

Prototyping

A prototype can be a scaled-down version of a subset of system functions used to verify or extend system requirements. It offers the opportunity to build a "proof of concept" version of an event-response for examination and verification by the user. A prototype can elicit changes in the initial perception of requirements or assist in the identification of new requirements. A team can build prototypes for just some of the more obscure event responses as another way of revealing essential system function.

The Focus of This Book

The focus of this book is on defining the requirements of an information system by using an event-driven strategy. Requirements form the foundation for subsequent phases of the life cycle and delivery process. If requirements are not correct, some part of the physical system will not meet user expectations and might not be used. By involving the user early with joint sessions (such as JAD) and by employing event analysis and event partitioning, conceptual models can often be developed more quickly than with earlier methods. The proposed system is viewed from multiple aspects, and a selective, iterative, and parallel approach is followed for the model building effort.

Many information systems are never implemented or never used after implementation owing primarily to poor user involvement resulting in poor system requirements. In response to this problem, this book focuses on the analysis and specification of information system requirements. Event-driven methods also offer many benefits in subsequent life cycle phases and for parallel tasks such as project management.

The concern of this book is "getting it right"—that is, defining an essential system that contains what is needed and nothing more. This book attacks two major problems: the communication of need by the user group and the complexity of the proposed system. Communication is enhanced because business events occur in the user's world and are a record of the business processes on a day-to-day basis. They are described in the user's own language. Complexity is managed since business events define system functions and system boundary early and partition the system into manageable, highly independent pieces; these pieces can be defined, designed, built, and implemented as separate subsystems. This event orientation and the resulting application partitioning affects the approach to requirements definition, influences the final system design, and facilitates and simplifies project management and system implementation.

This book also reveals an object orientation as a partitioning scheme conceptually rather than as a completely new way of building software. It is presented to show how responses to business events can be partitioned across object classes and how some of the models built in the event-partitioned approach can be reused. A more detailed discussion is included in Chapter 1.

As I examined the process of defining information system requirements, it seemed clear that conceptual modeling is vital to the discovery and specification process. My purpose for composing this book was to provide a condensed collection of information system modeling techniques that would be useful to professionals of information systems development. It also provides an introduction to an event-driven strategy for managers and users. This is a practical approach to analysis for *project managers, project leaders, analysts, designers,* and *analyst/programmers* who must be productive as well as effective and who are not tolerant of thousands of pages of methodology manuals.

Enterprise client/server systems will help IT deliver the expectations of the next decade. Since distributed applications as well as single processor applications need a conceptual base, the techniques presented in this book support current client/server efforts and also provide a foundation for evolving new methods.

Based on 34 years of IT experience and more than 10 years working with business events, I believe that an event-driven strategy for software development provides a more intuitive, effective partitioning of the user domain and the proposed system than other approaches, including object-oriented approaches. I have observed that, when used with joint design sessions such as JAD, events jumpstart the identification and specification of system requirements with early user involvement and improved user communication. And when combined with a spiral, incremental approach that dovetails with an architected RAD strategy, event-driven methods accelerate the delivery process. Event partitions persist throughout the delivery process and bring value to the entire development life cycle. When there is research to support the opinions expressed in this book, it will be so noted.

The methods presented here are not silver bullets, however; they will not solve all of the problems facing the software developer. But I and many other IT specialists believe that an event strategy solves many of the problems that plagued earlier methodologies. In the book *Yourdon Systems Method*, it is stated that time is more explicitly modeled in terms of events that occur in the environment of the system. Systems behave as they do only because of these events and the required policy for responding to them. Primarily, events separate functions into components that are activated at different times, with a simple interface between them. Real-world events and real-world entities provide objective rather than subjective techniques for identifying system requirements and are independent of preconceived ideas of the analyst [Yourdon, 1993].

The Organization of This Book

This book is divided into four major parts: *Part I: Business Events and System Development; Part II: Event-Partitioned System Requirements; Part III: Estimating Software Projects;* and *Part IV: Object-Partitioned Response to Events.*

Part I offers discussion on the nature of business events and their influence on the system development life cycle and is referential in nature. It focuses on partitioning of system requirements along with some advantages of event-based applications and effective user involvement. It provides information about the persistence of business events in the physical phases of the life cycle and in the supportive activities such as estimating and project management. Discussion is directed toward topics that must be understood if the techniques included in the book are to be of full value. Part I ends with a discussion of the effect of business events on development methodology and how it produces system design that is resilient to change.

Part II presents event-driven methods and techniques necessary for analyzing and specifying the requirements of an information system using models when possible. It presents the core modeling techniques of the event-oriented partitioning scheme and is designed for those defining system requirements and managing software development projects. At the beginning of Part II is a chapter (Chapter 4) that describes how a team might proceed through development of the deliverables. This chapter can be used to help define the tasks for use in project management. The next few chapters discuss methods for developing the various system models for the analysis and documentation of system requirements. Finally, system distribution is addressed with the development of data and event distribution tables. The techniques described here do not represent one particular commercial methodology but are a collection of "core techniques." Each chapter addresses and explores one technique and contains, as appropriate, discussions of purpose, description, and role, along with the following topics:

- Technique

- Example

- Risk if not completed

- Technique tips

A single case study is used throughout the book and is an abbreviated order processing system of the mail order, Internet type. It contains some inventory control functions but is not responsible for inventory replenishment.

Part III provides two chapters describing the function point estimating technique. Chapter 10 discusses the concepts and methods used, and Chapter 11 presents a detailed example.

Part IV discusses how responses to business events can be partitioned across object classes. It is not a methodology but instead teaches how event responses, discussed throughout Part II, can be developed in an object-oriented environment. Use cases are the typical mechanism for delivery of business events in an object-oriented environment, and event responses can be modeled initially as with an event-partitioned scheme. Part IV describes how required functionality can then be implemented as methods in object classes.

Appendix A presents a collection of examples from Part II. These examples are taken from the text and provide a single location in which to examine the system artifacts and their relationships to each other. The remaining appendices present explanations of the symbols used in the models of Part II and the General System Characteristics (GSC) tables for the IFPUG (International Function Point Users Group) function point counting methods.

How to Use This Book

As a guide, this book is not intended to provide pages and pages of discussion about each method as would a textbook. Instead, it is condensed to maximize its effectiveness and to use the analyst's time efficiently. It can be used to bring those trained in various methodologies to a single focus—that is, to give a team the same "playbook" and to bring the less experienced up to speed. It can also provide a review of techniques not recently used.

Part I provides foundational information. It will likely be read once and revisited occasionally but does not describe the methods for requirements definition. These chapters are recommended for, in addition to the developers, those who are not directly involved with the methodology, such as users and managers who want to understand the general principles being discussed.

Part II presents the methods for modeling and specifying a system's requirements. These chapters are designed for use by the analysis team during the definition of system requirements. I encourage you to record your experiences and document your ideas as you sharpen and refine your skills and discover new techniques. Thus the book can evolve and gain value in the hands of an experienced user over time.

Part III presents the function point project estimating techniques. It is intended to provide sufficient information about the function point counting practices to allow you to conduct a pilot case study to assess the effectiveness of the method. Function point analysis is based on the proposed system's requirements. The popularity of this technique is growing and may offer the best hope for a dependable estimating methodology.

Part IV discusses how a response to a business event can be object partitioned. It examines the reuse of much of the event-partitioned methods and then offers techniques for spreading the system functionality across object classes in an object-oriented environment.

It should be noted that when the term "phase" is used, it is not implied that these tasks are completed only once. They are part of an iterative approach that expects work to proceed from one set of tasks to another and to return to a phase as new understanding is gained. This book embraces the spiral model for the delivery process and will likely be less effective if used with a "waterfall" approach.

The same example case study is used throughout the book. This example system represents a catalogue-type Internet item ordering system that stores data about customers, items, and orders and processes order transactions. It does not address the typical custodial functions such as customer and item maintenance but focuses on the processing of customer orders, the reduction of inventory, the return of an item, and some decision support queries and reports.

This book is a guide. As such, it does not always offer as much explanation as some readers might need. A good reference for additional information is *Yourdon Systems Method: Model-Driven Systems Development* [Yourdon, 1993].

Business Events
and System Development

Part I provides concepts that are foundational to the understanding and use of the methods and techniques discussed in Parts II, III, and IV. The main theme is how business (domain) events affect the development life cycle and the delivery process and, most importantly, how events drive the system requirements methodology with a middle-out strategy. There are also discussions about the persistence of events throughout the delivery process and the critical nature of system requirements.

CHAPTER ONE

Foundational Concepts

1.1 The System Development Life Cycle

The process of systems analysis and physical design is the process of designing and building computer software that will model some set of business processes producing information that will serve the organization. All problem-solving approaches have an underlying life cycle. First it must be determined what is required, next a physical solution must be designed, and finally the solution is implemented. The software development life cycle is comprised of three major phases that parallel the components of any problem-solving effort: analysis, design, and construction.

Early software development methodologies followed the problem-solving life cycle in a waterfall fashion—that is, complete each phase before moving to the next, and don't look back. But each major phase is made up of numerous iterative tasks, and the process used to develop the system does not have to follow the life cycle in the waterfall approach. The system development life cycle phases are discussed below, but it must be remembered that the delivery process that will lead the developer through the life cycle is an iterative process and is the basis for the methods discussed in this book.

The analysis phase determines and documents *what* the system must accomplish. The design phase establishes *how* the computer system will function and the construction phase will *build* and test the resulting system. These phases are discussed below.

The *analysis phase* includes a preliminary investigation (some might consider this to be a separate, initial phase and not part of the analysis phase). This investigation must take a look at the purpose of the proposed system, study major objectives, and establish a preliminary scope so that the feasibility of the system can be examined. Once system feasibility is determined, system development can proceed. Otherwise, the life cycle ends when it is decided that the system will not be built at this time.

Once it has been decided to build the system, a team leader must be assigned and the development team formed. Specific member roles may be established at this time and schedules for each member can be considered. The first task of the team is to extend the preliminary investigation by completing the system charter—that is, the system purpose, system objectives, system critical success factors, and system nonobjectives that help establish system scope. Much of this work was completed during the preliminary study and the task now is to expand it by involving more of the user group and adding more detail. At any time, system feasibility can be challenged if new information and new perspectives make it questionable.

The most important of the analysis tasks is the definition of *system requirements*. The system requirements package answers the question "What must the system accomplish?" This is a nonphysical (conceptual) look at the proposed system. This effort is foundational and will have long-lasting effects on the remainder of the development effort. If not done well, it will negatively affect the outcome of the development effort since the wrong system will be developed. Most system failures, as discussed later, can be traced back to poor definition of the system requirements.

The *design phase* determines the physical composition of the system. It considers components such as system structure, screen and report design, database structure, security and control, and technology configurations. If the system requirements were not defined correctly, this effort will simply produce a very good system that will *not* meet the users' needs. This physical specification of the system becomes input to the next major phase—construction.

It is during the physical design phase that the development team might have the option of identifying and reusing existing system components. Often, the database CRUD functions (Create, Read, Update, and Delete) have been developed for other systems and can simply be assembled into the system solution.

It should be noted that the physical design of only selected partitions might be completed and passed on to construction, one by one, rather than completing the physical design of the entire system before moving ahead to construction. The development team might also choose a RAD approach for the system partitions—designing, building, and testing in a single pass.

During *construction,* the computer code will be purchased or developed and the system will undergo various levels of testing. Once the system is pronounced fit for user consumption, it will be put into production and the business converted to its use. These are not easy tasks and require hundreds or thousands of hours. The organization has invested a significant amount of resources in the development of the information system and is staking a part of its future on its operation. But no matter how well it has been designed and constructed, if the wrong system is built, it will not be used by the organization and the entire effort will have failed. *All phases subsequent to the definition of the system requirements depend on the correctness of that effort.*

1.2   The Critical Nature of Requirements

The goals of methodology have basically been the same for decades, to reduce the "time-to-market" and to produce a high-quality product (meets user expectations, easily maintainable, high performance). A requirements definition methodology must guide the analyst through the process of identifying and documenting the *required system components.* What are information system requirements and why are they important in the development of information systems?

1.2.1 What Are Requirements?

The primary product of the analysis phase is the set of system requirements. Webster defines a requirement as "something wanted or needed" [Webster's, 1994]. The definition of a *system requirement* must be more explicit than Webster's general definition.

System requirement. A function or capability that a system must have to provide needed business support for the users of the proposed system.

System requirement. (1) a condition or capability needed by a user to solve a problem or achieve an objective; (2) a condition or capability that must be met or possessed by a system (IEEE Standard 729,11).

System requirement. User needs plus set of all legal behaviors plus actual product's behavior [Davis, 1993].

The system requirements phase of the development life cycle answers the question "*what* must the system do?" It is a conceptual (nonphysical) look at the system. *How* the system will physically accomplish needed functionality is a matter for the subsequent physical design phase and should not be considered in this initial phase. Theoretically, there is only one set of requirements for a given system; there are typically many physical design configurations for its implementation (see Figure 1.1).

All system requirements combined will provide sufficient support for the user group to carry out their needed activities in the business area under study. As with other business costs, system functionality should be cost-effective and this cost feasibility should be a major factor in determining whether or not a function should be included in a proposed system. McMenamin and Palmer [1984] discuss false requirements. A system requirement is false if the system could fulfill its purpose without that requirement. A function that is irrelevant to the purpose of the system or one that is included solely to accommodate the anticipated technology to be used to implement the system is an example of a false requirement. Also, a requirement is false if it is described in such a way that makes the system do more than is necessary to accomplish the system's purpose.

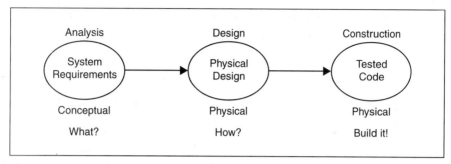

Figure 1.1   System development phases

1.2.2 Why Define Requirements?

Why spend time and effort on a phase of a system development project that produces no code? It is difficult to imagine someone beginning to build a house without a full set of plans. It is well known that a change after construction is underway is much more expensive than the same change made only in the plans.

The process of trying to define what an information system must do and at the same time design and construct the physical system components is not very efficient nor effective. This approach typically takes more time to produce a fully tested system and often leads to poor design. It is typically better to get to the "white board" before going to the keyboard. Most engineering disciplines model before they build. Considering their complexity and size, it would seem prudent to do the same when constructing information systems.

The dangers of false requirements are somewhat obvious. When system functionality is not included in the final version of a system, the system will not meet the needs and expectations of the users. If enough functionality is missed, the system may turn out to be totally unusable. Unneeded functionality, on the other hand, wastes organizational resources (both time and money), adds complexity to the system, and complicates development and maintenance.

In the early 1970s, three companies (GTE, TRW, and IBM) performed independent studies of the importance of requirements definition. These three companies reached the same basic results. They found that the effort required to detect and repair an error discovered during the coding phase was 5 to 10 times more costly than if that same error were detected and corrected in the requirements phase. When discovered in the maintenance phase, errors were up to 200 times more costly [Davis, 1993]. Even though the development environment is very different today, these principles still hold true.

Error Correction Compared with Requirements Phase

Coding Phase	Maintenance Phase
5–10 times more costly	Up to 200 times more costly

System requirements form the foundation of the system to be developed. An error or omission in this phase is propagated throughout the subsequent phases. Functions that are not needed will be built and important functions will be missed. With failure to satisfy user expectations as the most dominant problem in software development today [Lewis, 1996], defining the system requirements is considered by many to be the most critical phase of the development life cycle. The trick today is to minimize the time spent in this phase while completing it thoroughly.

1.3 Building the Right System

It was reported in *Object Magazine* [Lewis, 1996] that of some 250,000 development projects in 1995, one-third were canceled at a cost of $80 billion (U.S.), with an additional $60 billion estimated for cost overruns. As a result of discussions by 60 top U.S. IT managers, the principal conclusion was that a lack of user input represented a major contributory factor, and that particular key points were as follows.

- Lack of user involvement

- No clear statement of requirements

- No project ownership

- No clear vision and objectives

- Inadequate planning

- Overly ambitious milestones

- Lack of management support

1995 Information System Projects	
• Cost of canceled projects:	$80 billion
• Cost overruns:	$60 billion

In the article "Dirty Little Secrets" in the May 11, 1999, issue of *Intelligent Enterprise,* the authors state, "According to the most recent studies we've seen, somewhere around three-fourths of the new corporate software developed in the United States never goes into production. . . . For IT professionals, business requirements are at the heart of the problem. And we don't know how to do them." The challenge is to define the correct system requirements early in the delivery process and to minimize construction and postimplementation repair.

The days of freezing system requirements and then taking the next year or two to build the system are gone (it is questionable that those days should ever have occurred). With that mindset, it was ensured that the system would be one or two years old at conversion time. Today, much shorter delivery times, with incremental development and multiple releases, are recommended. This has been found to be one of the more successful implementation strategies and has become necessary with today's rapidly changing business environment. Once event-response subsystems have been identified, priorities can be set and applications composed of a subset of the event responses can be defined. Development and implementation can then proceed along those lines.

Building the right system begins with defining a set of true requirements—that is, those and only those that a system must have to fulfill its purpose. To accomplish this, the analysis team can define requirements based on real-world events and real-world entities that are relevant to the system under study. Then a process should be followed that provides for the verification of the requirements by iteration, review, and prototyping. The single most important aspect of defining accurate requirements is early and effective involvement of the subject-matter experts and users of the system. One technique that stands out as a way of accomplishing this is the use of joint design sessions. The remainder of this section is devoted to an overview of these sessions.

1.3.1 Joint Design Sessions

A Joint Application Workshop [JAW; often called Joint Design Session or Joint Application Design (JAD)] involving both the development team and the users strikes at the very heart of the problem of low user involvement. These sessions "harness the creativity and teamwork of group dynamics to define the users' view of the system" [August, 1991]. Ideas spawn new ideas and conflicts in business processes can be revealed and dealt with by the user group. When these sessions are facilitated properly and attended appropriately, they can both shorten the delivery process and increase the quality of the system requirements.

Users will typically learn about their colleagues and their business while ironing out necessary design issues and conflicts for the new system. System functionality is agreed on by the user group, and the analyst is given responsibility for modeling system requirements and for system architecture. The user becomes a key designer and owner of the system and therefore is expected to accept responsibility for its content. However, the user group must be dedicated and committed to this process if it is to be effective.

1.3.2 Session Facilitation

Sessions must be led by an experienced facilitator with the power to make session decisions. A Joint Application Workshop is not just a meeting of the minds but is a mindset as well, and participants must put organizational goals ahead of their own. The topics in these sessions must be carefully "time boxed" and the number of sessions determined by need rather than by management dictate.

But JAWs add yet another challenge to the management effort. The same dynamics that make them so valuable also make them difficult to control and manage. First of all, getting a dozen or more users away from their work and in the same room at the same time for a significant amount of time is not easy. This is one reason to time box the sessions and publish the schedule. When users attend, they expect to discuss the part of the system for which they have responsibility and expertise. Issues can always be rescheduled and revisited. However, the purpose of the sessions is to discover requirements, so some flexibility in schedule may be required. An experienced facilitator will know when guidelines and schedules must be temporarily abandoned to best accomplish the session goals.

> **Time box.** The relatively ridged time period or amount of time planned for an activity. The time box is not violated; even if discussion is not completed, the session moves on to another topic and another session is scheduled to complete unresolved issues. Of course, in practice, it may be better to slip a time box.
>
> **Example:** An evening TV newscast must go on at the specified time; time to prepare is "time boxed" and there is no extension.

Secondly, managing a meeting that has so many contributors, often disagreeing with each other, can be difficult. It is a real challenge to keep the sessions on schedule and on track and still hear from all those that have relevant contributions. Formal facilitator training is available and will typically have positive payback for the effort and expense.

The responsibility for conflict resolution and session attendance lies with the user groups. The JAW's facilitator must know when to end a discussion and then assign responsibility for resolution by a specific date to a designated user. The time required for the joint sessions must be allocated, expected, and fully supported by upper management. The user groups typically cannot be expected to work these sessions into their schedules on their own.

1.3.3 Participation Roles

Judy August [1991] defines six roles for joint design sessions, five of which are listed below.

- Executive sponsor
- Session leader
- Analyst
- User representative
- Specialist

A role can be filled by one or more persons, and more than one role can be performed by a single person. The role of user representative is typically filled by more than one person, whereas a user representative could also be a specialist.

Peter Coad, CEO of Object International, in his newsletter of June 10, 1997, lists several roles and responsibilities for the design working sessions that his company uses on projects. The facilitator should

- Remain neutral

- Get and enforce agreements

- Help group focus

- Protect ideas from attack

- Ensure opportunity to participate

- Write main ideas

Each group member should

- Focus on task

- Listen to understand

- Contribute ideas

- State concerns openly

1.3.4 Number of Participants

How many participants can an effective session include? Since all the participants need to be heard and since the participants often don't agree on the topic of discussion, no more than about a dozen should be in the session room at one time. Observers whose objective is to learn about the new system can also attend as long as they are not expected to contribute. A schedule of each session, with the topics to be discussed, should be published so that only those participants with relevant information to share will attend as contributors.

1.3.5 Session Objectives

"Although a [Joint Design Session] captures the information needed to perform the technical development tasks (i.e., database and program design, coding and testing), it stops short of actually accomplishing them. These tasks will be performed subsequent to the [joint] effort by a technical team." The joint design groups typically reflect the levels and departments of the organization that the system will serve. Individuals ranging from the highest levels of the organization to the data entry operator may share ideas about the system [August, 1991].

A software design joint session has five major objectives [August, 1991].

- Define detailed requirements and scope.

- Design screen and report layouts.

- Capture edit, validation, processing, and interface requirements.

- Develop the prototype.

- Complete and obtain approval of the joint session document.

JAWs can accelerate the analysis and design process and they can also result in higher-quality systems through the group dynamics that they employ and a high level of user involvement.

1.4 Verifying System Requirements

With the staggering losses that occur in software development as a result of poor requirements, as reported in Section 1.3, it is important not only to establish effective methods for the initial requirements gathering effort but also to adopt effective verification techniques. There is no silver bullet, no software package that can ensure that no requirements are missed and that no false requirements are defined. The most effective way to avoid inaccurate requirements is to use well-facilitated, well-attended joint requirements gathering sessions, as described in the preceding section. The group dynamics will challenge and verify the requirements as they are developed in a spiral, iterative fashion. The following discussion explores some of the other mechanisms for requirements verification.

1.4.1 Partitioning

The partitioning of a system that results from a business event strategy provides some real benefits for verification of the requirements. One of the main problems faced in the effort to develop an information system is the high level of complexity that is inherent in the business problem and also in the interaction of the software and hardware components. This complexity impacts the requirements gathering effort and then complicates attempts to verify the resulting requirements package. Business events provide an intuitive, real-world look at a system's requirements that are partitioned into relatively small, highly cohesive units. This allows the analysis team to address one event response unit at a time and focus on verification of a tightly defined part of the business with the domain experts.

The modeling techniques examine the proposed system from multiple aspects. While a bit redundant, this provides multiple opportunities to recognize false requirements, detect missing requirements, and verify true requirements. Models such as the event diagram force the investigation to a level of detail that also aids in the verification of the requirements. The very process of examining a problem at levels of greater detail forces a more thorough understanding.

1.4.2 Iteration

When joint sessions are used to define system requirements, verification takes place as the team iterates through the analysis and specification tasks. Each time requirements are put before the user group for further fleshing out, work already completed is scrutinized and verified. This spiral approach places the documentation before the domain experts over and over again, each time based on a greater understanding of the system.

1.4.3 Prototyping

Some of the more complex or obscure event responses can be prototyped to reveal missing or false requirements and to verify the true requirements. These prototypes can be run in a joint session or demonstrated to individual domain experts. Prototyping can include screen mockups, but such mockups often don't thoroughly represent the processing and offer limited value for verification. Whatever the mechanism, user interfaces, business rules for data transformation, and stored data updates must all be verified.

1.4.4 Review Sessions

Sessions designed specifically for verification can be scheduled on an event-by-event basis. These sessions can focus on users or can be analysis team walkthroughs.

1.4.5 Testing

Unit, integration, and system testing do not verify the correctness of system requirements. These tests simply verify that the requirements, correct or incorrect, have been developed as specified and that the software runs without errors.

The only tests designed to verify requirements are the user acceptance tests (UATs). These tests are based on the requirements and are used to verify that the correct software has been developed. The problem with discovering errors at this point in the development life cycle is that the UAT occurs after development and is much too late. Errors need to be discovered during the conceptual modeling phase when the cost of repair is the lowest.

> **Unit testing.** The testing of individual programs, program modules, and special library routines.
>
> **Integration testing.** The testing of programs as they interface as a system.
>
> **System testing.** The testing of integrated programs in a production environment.

1.5 Why Business Events?

One problem that is typically faced during software development is the difficulty in communication that results from the differences in the backgrounds of the users and the development team, along with a lack of understanding by the user group of exactly what the system must do. This chasm makes accurate understanding and documentation of user expectations and system requirements a difficult challenge and one that often is not met.

A second problem is the complexity of the proposed system. This complexity is largely due to system size and the interactions among system components. It must be managed by some scheme of "divide and conquer."

The concept of business events was formally introduced by McMenamin and Palmer in their 1984 book *Essential Systems Analysis*. Business events bring relief to both problems cited above.

Business events happen in the user's world. They are external to the system and are the intuitive activities that users experience on a day-to-day basis. They

> **Event.** "An event is some change in the system's environment" [McMenamin and Palmer, 1984].
>
> **Business event.** An activity in the user's environment that requires a response from the proposed information system.
>
> **Screen event.** An activity such as the clicking of a command button in a screen window that invokes some action from the software. Screen events are not related to business events and will not be referred to further in this book.

are described in the business language of the user, and they partition the system for subsequent development tasks (see Figures 1.2 and 1.5).

"The events that a system responds to are of two types: external events, which are initiated by entities in the environment and temporal events, which are initiated by the passing of time" [McMenamin and Palmer, 1984] or by the occurrence of a specified time.

When business events are used as the primary partitioning scheme, the entire methodology is affected because everything that is done subsequent to the initial partitioning can be applied to a single partition at a time. With event partitioning, each partition is highly independent and remains recognizable to the user as well as the developer as it persists throughout the development process. Many of these partitions tend to be relatively simple database access functions and can be prototyped and developed in a shorter time period, making management of the development process easier.

Alan Davis describes another problem the analyst often encounters when defining conceptual system requirements. He points out how perspective can determine whether functionality is described by "what" the system is to do (conceptual) or "how" the system will do it (physical) [Davis, 1993].

Conceptual:
- Nonphysical
- "Order" rather than "mail order" or "telephone order"
- Elementary business process rather than a computer program

Physical:
- Screen design
- Which type of computer and where the computers will be located
- Programs and languages

It is the strategy of this book to define requirements conceptually rather than physically. Using business events for initial description of needed system functionality moves the perspective outside of the boundary of the proposed system and into the business environment. This reduces the chances that system requirements will contain physical components, because the description of event responses is considered independently.

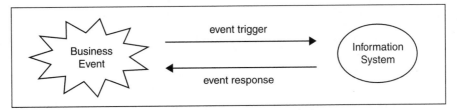

Figure 1.2   Business events and system response

Yet another set of problems, related to earlier methodologies, is described in *Yourdon Systems Method* [Yourdon, 1993].

- Analysis-paralysis: Correct partitioning of the system cannot be completed until the system is understood, and the system cannot be understood until it has been effectively partitioned.

- Analyst bias: Top-down functional decomposition is a creative technique and reflects the way the analyst perceives the system. This bias is not easily removed.

- Fragmentation of policy: It is sometimes found that related functions were widely separated in the proposed system model, causing difficulty in verification.

To avoid these problems, event-driven analysis techniques are based on real-world requirements—that is, business events and business entities. System function and system data are considered equally. The partitioning approach is middle-out; it starts with intuitive, recognizable business events and entities and aggregates upward and decomposes downward. Related functions are encapsulated in a single response to an event benefiting both the definition and verification processes.

Some of the business benefits that can be realized from an event-based methodology are listed below.

- User involvement and improved user communication

- Consistency of methods from project to project

- Incremental implementation

- Resiliency and response to change

- Application across multiple system types

- Persistence of the underlying strategy across all phases of the development life cycle

The event strategy is not limited to business systems. In the business system example used in this book, the system responds to the submission of an order or the return of a previously purchased item. But in a more scientific application, the receipt of a radar signal could invoke a response from the system, and for a real-time system the trigger could be a change in a continuous stream of paint flow data in an automatic painting system. An event strategy can be applied to any proposed system that must respond to some activity or event that occurs in the problem domain.

The methods and techniques presented in this book are highly influenced by the concept of business events, and event partitioning is the major theme throughout. The pervasive nature of business events will provide benefits to the entire requirements effort as well as subsequent development phases.

1.6 Business Events and System Requirements

1.6.1 Business Events and the User

When business events are defined early in the requirements phase, the users' first experience with the development effort is on their own turf rather than in the "computer guy's world." They have control of both the language and the system definition since they are describing what they do in their own language.

When joint design sessions are being used, the users should outnumber the developers and should not feel threatened by the process. Business events tend to invite the user on-board the system development effort early and attack the very heart of the user/developer communication problem.

1.6.2 Business Events and the System Response

Systems that respond to business events are referred to by McMenamin and Palmer as *planned response systems.* An agent of the system's environment acts on the system, and the system reacts to the external agent. Whenever a specific business event occurs, a related set of actions is performed by the information system.

For an *external business event,* some change in the system's environment occurs and sends an event trigger to the system. The part of the system dedicated to responding to the business event is in an idle state, reacts to the trigger by completing all of the required processing and producing the required output, and returns to an idle state. It is an elementary process and must leave the business in a consistent state. The processing invoked by an external event can be represented by Figure 1.3 (also refer to Appendix B, Model Notation and Symbol).

For a *temporal business event,* a point in time is reached. The part of the system dedicated to responding to that business event executes and completes all of the processing required and returns to an idle state. As with an external event, it must leave the business in a consistent state. Temporal event processing can be represented by Figure 1.4.

Note in Figure 1.4 that there is no trigger shown incoming to the process since time has been the activating trigger. This is a common signature for Data Flow Diagrams (DFDs) when representing temporal events. However, some modelers use a broken-line control flow for temporal triggers.

A third type of event, called a *state event,* is typically found in real-time systems. State events invoke processing based on a change in system state, such as in an elevator control system or an automatic painting system. This type of system is also a "planned response" system (as described in this book) and can be modeled

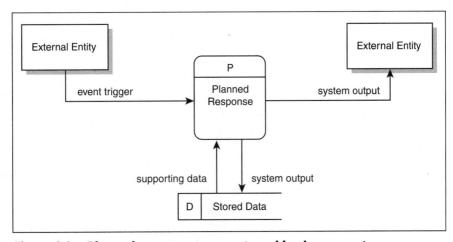

Figure 1.3   Planned response to an external business event

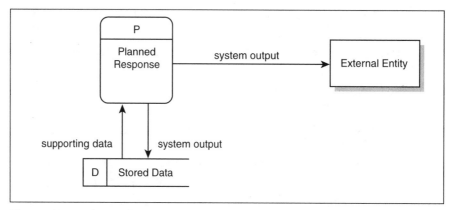

Figure 1.4   Planned response to a temporal business event

in a manner similar to external and temporal events. State event triggers are typically depicted with a broken-line control flow.

By definition of events and event responses, there are no internal events that trigger additional system processing. Any function that can respond immediately to the processing of an event response is, by definition, part of that response. Any function that responds to the processing of an event response in a delayed fashion is responding to a trigger from one of the three types of events and is an event response in its own right.

Business information systems usually respond to external and temporal events. These two types of events will be the focus of the methods presented in this book.

Each business event (external and temporal) and the resulting planned response begin to partition the proposed system into manageable pieces very early in the requirements definition phase (see Figure 1.5). These pieces (system partitions) have some compelling properties. They are highly independent subsystems because they interface with only the external environment and stored data. By definition, they do not interact directly with other event responses. Also, for most business applications, a high percentage of these partitions are typically relatively simple custodial accesses or updates to the database.

These partitions affect requirements definition, system design, system construction, and project management. They facilitate the definition of requirements by focusing on activities found in the user environment. They influence system design and construction by partitioning the system into highly independent subsystems. They simplify project management by allowing the allocation of resources to relatively simple, highly cohesive subsystems.

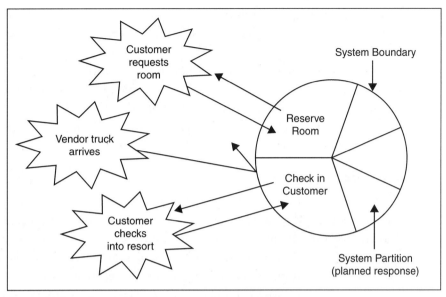

Figure 1.5   Planned response system partitions

1.6.3 Business Events and Data

Business events and a system's data, and thus the data model, are tightly coupled because stored data has value only when it is used—that is, processed to generate an output product. The state of a data entity (an object class in an object orientation) changes in response to an event. For example, when the event "customer reserves a room" occurs in a resort management system, the state of that room changes from "available" to "reserved." The state changes again when the customer checks into or out of the resort. In the data model fragment that represents the customer entity and the room entity, these events represent a relationship between the two data entities (see Figure 1.6). In this case, the many-to-many

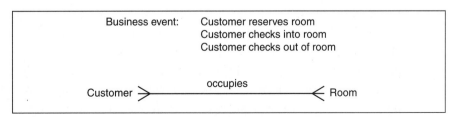

Figure 1.6   Business events and entity relationships

cardinality will require resolution later in the delivery process, but early in the requirements definition phase it most accurately represents the business under study.

The business event list contains a plethora of information about both data entities and the relationships that will be documented in the data model. The business events begin to reveal much about the data that will be needed to support the required processing and generation of system outputs by the system event responses.

1.6.4 Partitioning an Event Response

To be useful to the design effort, the required processing of an event response should be specified in sufficient detail to be verifiable by the user while the user is closely involved with the requirements definition task. When the event-partitioning scheme is used throughout the life cycle, this specification can typically be accomplished by using structured English and by separately documenting user interfaces, database interfaces, and business rules. This begins to prepare for distribution across a multiple-tier technical configuration.

When an object-oriented approach is followed, each event response will be decomposed first into the object classes that will collaborate to provide the system response. The processing documentation must then identify the user and database interfaces along with the business rules for the event response under study and must allocate these components to the appropriate object classes. These object classes might already exist since an object class is obligated to serve multiple systems and subsystems.

Event response specifications are not at a program code level; they document the processing needed. If the development team wants more detailed specifications, they will be generated during the physical design effort.

1.7 System Partitioning

One of the biggest problems faced by analysts during the early stages of the system development process is breaking the proposed system into manageable pieces. This partitioning scheme should produce relatively small, independent subsystems that will support subsequent life cycle efforts. Early methodologies as well as some more recent ones decompose from the top down. Most of these partitioning schemes result in system components that have high coupling—that is, significant dependence on each other that increases the development and management effort throughout the development life cycle.

The initial partitioning of a system is one of the more important activities of analysis. These partitions will positively or negatively affect the entire development effort. The partitioning of systems has its roots in problem-solving theory—that is, in the concept of "divide and conquer." Most systems that are dealt with today are much too big to design and build as one piece. But the very nature and complexity of an information system provides for many ways in which it can be partitioned into basic elements. The reader's attention is directed to Figure I.2 in the subsection Partitioning Schemes under Modern System Development Methods with Events, in the Introduction.

1.7.1 Partitioning: An Event Orientation

Work done at the University of California at Berkeley by Eleanor Rosch has demonstrated that humans typically don't categorize and classify from the top down [DeSmedt, 1994]. They instead begin at a level somewhere in the middle with those things with which they are most familiar. When a system is partitioned using events, something very similar is accomplished. The beginning is somewhere in the middle of the hierarchy with familiar user activities, and the model is synthesized upward and decomposed downward as needed, a process referred to as "middle out."

"An event is some change in the system's environment, and a response is the set of actions performed by the system whenever a certain event occurs." [McMenamin and Palmer, 1984] This set of actions or set of system instructions is an *event response* and is the basis for the partitioning of the system. By definition, all processing in response to a business event is continual (this does not mean that the system cannot pause) and must be accomplished before the event response becomes idle again awaiting another arrival of its trigger.

This offers an approach that produces partitions with relatively low coupling; data is exchanged only with external agents and data stores and not directly with another partition. The coupling occurs only through the stored data component of the system.

> **To partition by events.** To divide the system into major components based on the system's response to business events. Each event response is a system partition.

This is a very powerful paradigm because the resulting independence of the partitions allows for flexibility in the assignment of priorities and development teams and also aids in other project management activities since each partition is a subsystem to be managed separately. Another important aspect of the approach is that each subsystem is described in the user's language from the user's perspective in the early stages of the analysis process.

This is not a top-down approach in which the system is viewed as a single entity and then successively decomposed until an adequate level of detail is obtained. Event-driven partitions are derived at the middle of the hierarchy and then synthesized upward to the context diagram and decomposed downward to reach the necessary processing detail.

The decomposition is controlled by necessity, not by rule. Custodial database functions such as Create, Read, Update, and Delete (CRUD) typically need not be modeled any further than the event response level and a few lines of structured English. These functions, along with typical user interface functions, can be prototyped using a fourth-generation language with a user as a close team member. In fact, many have probably been done before and can be reused. Only the partitions with complexity or functionality unfamiliar to the developers need be decomposed diagrammatically.

With this approach, an event list is developed depicting the business area events to which the system must respond. These events occur in the user's domain and are described in the user's language. The user participates significantly in the identification of the events. The system partitions derived from these business events persist from requirements definition through construction and testing and can be managed and developed independently on the basis of data dependencies and priorities.

1.7.2 Partitioning: An Object Orientation

As more and more systems follow a distributed architecture, objects become more and more attractive. In some ways, object classes *distribute more cleanly* than other types of partitions because the data and the processing are bundled together into object classes. An object-oriented approach also provides for a type of *reuse* that is not available in a traditional approach. The hierarchical nature of object classes allows for both data and process properties to be handed down to lower-level classes. So, by placing a new object class into the hierarchy, all properties above the new class in the same hierarchical path are "reused" and immediately available. (The fact that an object class already exists in the development environment contributes little more to reuse than the traditional library routines have in the past. With existing object classes, it is likely that new methods, or functions, will need to be added to support a new application just as with library routines.)

However, an object orientation also brings with it some problems. In an event orientation, the response to a business event is natural and in fact determines the system-partitioning scheme for the entire application. However, with an object orientation, the event response is very different from the system partitioning that occurs by object class. After business events are considered (typically as use cases) early in the analysis phase, a significant change is made when the system-partitioning scheme becomes a set of object classes. But the responses to the business events by collaboration between object classes must still be maintained, because this is the operation of the system that the user expects and needs. This requirement to maintain two perspectives (events for the user interface and object classes for the major system-partitioning scheme) adds complexity to that already inherent in the business problem.

Use case. A behaviorally related sequence of steps (a scenario), both automated and manual, for the purpose of completing a single business task [Whitten and Bentley, 1998].

Use case modeling. The process of identifying and modeling business events, who initiated them, and how the system responds to them [Whitten and Bentley, 1998].

And what about *maintenance* of an object-oriented application? In an object-oriented approach, a change in an application will likely involve more than one partition (object class), even when the business change affects only one business event. The collaboration between object classes to support a response to a business event is what must be considered when the changing business requires change in the information system. This is very different from an event-partitioned system, in which, by its very nature, the change is likely to be isolated to a single partition.

Another concern is that when an object class is selected for distribution to a separate physical location, its entire inheritance structure must also be distributed. This could result in data and processes being distributed unnecessarily.

CHAPTER TWO

The Pervasive Nature of Business Events

- 2.1 Partitioning the Physical System
- 2.2 The Physical Distribution of Business Events
- 2.3 Business Events and Project Management
- 2.4 Business Events and Estimating Project Size

Traceability refers to the capability of linking code with the requirement from which it originated. With some of the decomposition schemes used in the past, this was no easy task. With a business event-partitioning approach, events and event responses can be identified throughout the different levels of the life cycle and typically are visible in the final system/user interface. They also have an impact on the distribution and implementation of the application, and they influence many of the project support activities such as project estimating and project management.

2.1 Partitioning the Physical System

We have heard for decades just how difficult and unnatural was the transition from an analysis network model to the physical design structure models of the early structured design methodologies. Peter Coad offers one solution to this problem in his object-oriented analysis and design methodology. It does not make a model switch but instead adds layers of detail as work moves from the conceptual to the physical.

One of the benefits of event partitioning is that the event responses are *highly independent subsystems* coupled only through the database. The data dependencies are documented in the interaction model and influence the priority of subsystem development as the system transitions from conceptual requirements to a physical configuration. As development moves through the physical tasks, the event-response subsystems remain independent. The design team works with the business events that were identified by the user in the earliest tasks of the project and still remain intact. This brings familiarity, consistency, and control to the project.

Physical Development Life Cycle Phases
  Physical design
  Construction
  Testing
  Implementation
  Maintenance

Physical specifications evolve readily from the structured English generated for each event response. Screen and report design follows along the lines of the business events. Prototyping decisions can be made and security and control issues can be considered on a subsystem-by-subsystem basis. Construction and testing as well as design tasks can also be assigned by event response, and when maintenance is needed, it too will often fall along partitioning lines.

Another of the attractive properties of business events is the *persistence* of the event partitions, as can be seen from the discussion of partition independence in Section 1.7. These partitions tend to persist throughout the development life cycle (see Table 2.1) and affect not only the requirements definition but also system design, construction and implementation, and project management. Experience at Taylor University [Wiley, 1995] has shown that, in most cases, business events end up as menu options in the user interface of the finished system described in the language of the user group. This facilitates the traceability of system requirements that is required by many organizations and by some government contracts. Since most of these partitions tend to be relatively small, and since the partitions originated in the system requirements (and in fact were derived from the business events), the effort of tracing a component of code back to its root requirement is straightforward.

**Table 2.1. Partition Persistence Throughout the
Development Life Cycle**

Development Phases			
Requirements	Design	Construction	Maintenance
Produce	Menu option,	Code and	Update
Account	screens, security	test *PAB*	code for
Balance	for *PAB*		*PAB*

"Produce Account Balance" (PAB) persists through all development phases.

2.2 The Physical Distribution of Business Events

A distributed system consists of multiple components running on multiple processors working together to support the information needs of an organization. This implies that the data and processes will be distributed over several processors and in many cases over multiple geographic locations, introducing a number of design and control complications. In the ideal distributed system, the data and processing are located in the most efficient location. A very sophisticated system infrastructure is needed to make such an ideal system possible. Distributed systems tend to be more complex and more difficult to manage. So why not implement all systems on a single processor such as a mainframe?

2.2.1 The Business Challenge

The business environment of the 1990s (and beyond) is competitive, fast-paced, and constantly changing. To meet the demands of this marketplace, businesses must perform at ever higher levels, increasing their productivity and quality while maintaining profitability. An organization's mean time to market with new products and services is likely to be a key factor to its success or failure. Products are being built from components assembled from various plants, sometimes even the plants of competitors. Orders must be filled, not within days but within hours or minutes. [August, 1991]

Increasing revenue is one measure of success. But another measure is profit margin. Companies today are striving to do more with less. Organizational hierarchies are being flattened. Processes are being streamlined or fundamentally re-engineered. Employees are being empowered, not just to act, but to make decisions about what actions to take, especially when interacting directly with customers. One aspect of this empowerment occurs through changes in company policies—employees' jobs are being redefined to encompass greater authority and greater responsibilities. Another aspect of the empowerment is dependent on improved or increased automation. [Bohl, 1995]

Many organizations are finding that their current business systems are inadequate to support current and future business needs, and they are making major business changes. Many of these organizations are turning to information technology to support the new business processes. These new systems must be

- Scalable (expandable to more powerful hardware platforms; to hundreds or even thousands of users)

- Flexible (able to adjust to business and technology changes)

- High performance (able to make use of the latest technology in the right place)

- Easy to use with rich user interfaces (able to take advantage of Graphical User Interface front ends)

- Vendor independent (able to use many different platforms)

- Able to access legacy mainframe system data

A distributed system architecture, such as Client/Server, is most often the better choice to meet these system requirements.

2.2.2 System Complexity

When parts of a system are distributed, especially into n-tier architectures, the complexity of the system increases significantly. The distribution of a system may introduce multiple servers on different machines running different operating systems and multiple Database Management Systems, all from multiple vendors. Over time, the distributed configuration of a partitioned system will likely need to be changed as an organization's business needs and technology options change.

Other considerations are more subtle. For example, an application developer constructing an application to run on a single machine may assume that communications between components are enacted as simple call statements, and that any message (call) sent by one component will be received successfully by the component to which it is sent. In a distributed application, the communications may be implemented as messages that travel long distances over wires or cable with a resultant higher likelihood of failure. The developer may choose to include additional error handling logic to provide for such possibilities. [Bohl, 1995]

2.2.3 Distribution of Event Responses

As an information system becomes more and more fragmented in the *n*-tier architectures, having a stable, conceptual model of the system developed during analysis that is not affected by the changing physical configuration becomes increasingly important. This model can be used as the root for physical system configuration derivation, and regardless of the dynamic nature of the physical system, can offer a stable representation of the system requirements.

Systems tend to distribute naturally along the lines of business events. Ask users what part of a system they need at their locations and they will typically describe the functions they need rather than the data or the objects. These requests for functionality can and should drive the distribution of the system. Once the distribution of events is set, it is a simple task to identify the required data or object classes from the event diagrams.

2.3 Business Events and Project Management

An important aspect of project management is the allocation of resources to tasks; resources are people and time and may be constrained by budget requirements. The project tasks that are scheduled and to which resources are allocated come from the methodology being used for the project, whether or not that methodology is a formal one.

Project management can be positively or negatively affected by the way the system is originally partitioned. When the components of a system fail to follow along the lines of the business and fail to persist throughout the development life cycle, project management is fragmented and becomes more difficult. On the other hand, when the system is partitioned by business events, the design and development tasks are natural and will be around when the system is finally constructed and delivered. This tightly couples project management and the methodology being used. Table 2.2 illustrates how a single business event is the focus of tasks throughout the delivery process.

Table 2.2.　Business Event Focus Throughout Delivery Process

Physical Design Deliverables					
Business Event	System Response	Screen and Report Design	Prototype	Security and Control	Allocation to Physical Processors
Customer Requests Account Balance	*Produce Account Balance*	for *Produce Account Balance*	for *Produce Account Balance*	for *Produce Account Balance*	Distribute *Produce Account Balance*

Physical design tasks applied to one event response

2.3.1　What Is a Project?

A software development project is a set of activities that starts and ends at identifiable points in time and that produces quantifiable and qualifiable software deliverables. Along the way, other deliverables will be produced, many in the form of human- and machine-readable documentation. These interim deliverables help to monitor progress of the project, and some of them will form permanent components of the total software package. . . .

So, developing the first deliverable version of an application system for a customer or user is a project. Making a set of specific changes to an existing application or operating system can also be defined as a project. [King, 1992]

This guide focuses on projects whose main objectives relate to the building of a new software application. It relies heavily on business events for the initial partitioning of the system and for Joint Application Workshops (JAWs) and can accelerate the identification and documentation of system requirements.

2.3.2　Project Failures

Why do projects fail? David King puts it this way:

As we have all seen, many system development projects fail, as measured by one criterion or another. I define a project as having failed if it fails to meet the user's minimum requirements, or is implemented too late to be effective, or exceeds its development or operational budget by an unacceptable amount.

There are sometimes purely political reasons for project failures, and these are usually the most unpredictable and least preventable. Nevertheless, for these and other reasons, software projects do fail. . . . Some preventable reasons for project failure include the following:

1. Lack of clear, understandable specifications
2. Poor documentation
3. Poor communications
4. Overambitious objectives
5. Low quality, poor performance
6. Never-ending development
7. High costs and cost overruns
8. Perpetual maintenance [King, 1992]

2.3.3 Project Failure Rates

A successful project must produce a system that satisfies the user or user management, meets the needs of the business area under study, is within schedule and budget, is relatively error-free, and is easily maintained.

Capers Jones reports a study that shows the approximate frequencies of various kinds of software project outcomes, ranging from early completion to total cancellation. The study examined six different project sizes; the results are shown in Table 2.3 [Jones, 1998]. The complexity of a software system increases exponentially as the size increases. It can easily be seen from the table that the larger projects are much more likely to produce unsuccessful results than are the smaller ones.

2.3.4 Improved Project Management

While allocation of resources to tasks and the scheduling of those tasks are vital to the success of project management, definition of the tasks in the first place is even more important. These tasks should be the products of the development methodology and the team's decisions regarding which deliverables will be produced. Since the methodology presented in this book is a "toolbox" of deliverables, some tasks may not be cost-effective for any particular project. This guide will identify and describe each of the tasks and deliverables for an event-driven development life cycle and present the risk of their omission.

Table 2.3.   Project Outcome Probability

Project Size (function points)	Probability of Selected Outcomes, %			
	Early	On Time	Delayed	Canceled
1	14.68	83.16	1.92	0.25
10	11.08	81.25	5.67	2.00
100	6.06	74.77	11.83	7.33
1,000	1.24	60.76	17.67	20.33
10,000	0.14	28.03	23.83	48.00
100,000	0.00	13.67	21.33	65.00

Most application systems are very complex and too large to approach as single components. A system must be broken into many smaller pieces if its development is to be controlled and managed. The method used for the original partitioning of the system will affect the entire project from beginning to end and will affect how the system is viewed from analysis to testing to maintenance. The partitions should persist throughout the development life cycle.

A good foundational analysis phase sets the tone for the remainder of the project and partitions the project management effort as well as the application system. Using business events as the basis for partitioning is proving to be superior for accelerating development and for maintaining system quality. This method not only has many advantages for software development but also partitions the management effort and makes management and control of the project easier.

Project management is secondary to the actual development of the system. The project management effort essentially fits around the system development effort and depends on it for its structure. There is a significant project management advantage when the partitioning scheme follows the natural components of the business that is being modeled, especially when that structure is traceable throughout the entire project and is easily discernible in the final software product. Event partitioning does all of the above and thus supports both the development of the system and the management of the project. Throughout Part II, project management activities and tips will be presented in independent windows as appropriate. They will follow the format shown in this box.

Project Management Tips

- Schedule joint session to develop business event list.
- Allow 3–4 hours; attendance, 10–12 users.
- Do not attempt to define system responses to the events.

2.4 Business Events and Estimating Project Size

The estimation of a software project (both schedule and budget) has historically been difficult and has been a problem for most teams. The average duration of a project today is reported to average more than two times the original estimate. Much of the problem is that system requirements are often poorly defined and thus estimates are made without a complete understanding of the system to be built. If a system is not fully understood, it cannot be estimated accurately. Another problem is that the software industry has never found a dependable method for estimating. Capers Jones lists the following three general types of manual estimating methods in use today [1998].

- Project-level estimates using rules of thumb

- Phase-level estimates using ratios and percentages

- Activity-level estimates using work-breakdown structures

However, with the dynamic nature of today's business and the complexity of today's systems, many of them distributed, these methods can produce significant errors. *Rules of thumb* is one of the oldest methods and is still widely used today. An example might be that applications average 500 lines of code per staff-month. After estimating the lines of code for the project, needed resources could be projected. *Ratios and percentages* is another of the older methods and applies percentages to remaining phases of the project based on the sizes of completed phases. For example, if analysis takes one month, the remaining project phases will take nine times that long, or an additional nine months. A third type of estimating technique is done at the *activity or task level*. The project is broken down into dozens of activities, and each task is estimated separately. This is a very time-consuming method but is also the most accurate. An example might be estimating the resources needed to design a screen for "Return Item."

None of the methods discussed above is based on the requirements of the proposed system. These methods depend on the commonality of projects and systems along with lines-of-code standards to arrive at project size. Function Point Analysis (FPA) is a method that uses system requirements as its foundation. Five specific system components along with 14 general system characteristics are evaluated and weighted to determine a total function point count. A standard metric is then applied to the count to arrive at project size. This method is supported by an international users group and is continuously refined and updated.

An event-driven approach to the definition of system requirements provides most of the components needed to do FPA. The models developed expose system elements that are used in the counting of function points. Since the system is partitioned by events and models are completed for each event response, estimates can be made and modified on an event-by-event basis. Incremental releases as well as the total system can be estimated. FPA is based on the definition of elementary processes that map very closely to the event diagrams of the methodology presented in this book.

Events not only persist throughout the development life cycle phases and in the software products but also affect many of the project's cross-life-cycle activities such as those found in project management and project estimation.

CHAPTER THREE

Business Events
and Methodology

- 3.1 **Middle-Out Strategy**
- 3.2 **Conceptual Models and the Reduced Role of the DFD**
- 3.3 **Business Events and RAD**
- 3.4 **Responding to Change**
- 3.5 **Adopting an Event-Driven Approach for Your Organization**
- 3.6 **Methodology Overview**

Many organizations are scrambling to find new ways of doing business to improve their competitive positions, and to lower costs and increase productivity. In many of these cases, Information Technology (IT) is playing a major role. It has become critical that new information systems be developed to meet user and enterprise needs, be built quickly, and be designed so as to be readily extendable to meet future business challenges. Many of the older methods cannot compete in today's business environment. They expend resources on artifacts that don't provide good returns on investment, they do not promote user participation, and, because they follow a rigid waterfall approach, they don't respond well to change. Major system efforts must be partitioned into projects of months, not years, and must use the newest methods such as prototyping and distributed system architectures. Methodologies that support these new approaches are vital to the successful development of these mission-critical systems.

With the use of joint design sessions involving both the development team and the user community, along with an *event orientation* and simplified event diagrams, the analysis process can be accelerated and at the same time be more effective. The system is partitioned into subsystems that can be modeled independently and in parallel. These constructs persist through design and construction and aid in project management and control. For a typical database-centered system, fourth-generation language prototyping of a large percentage of the system is possible with the conceptual models that are built.

With the increased use of distributed systems architecture, primarily client/server, *object-oriented* implementations have become very popular because objects have some distribution advantages. Many of the models and techniques can be common to both traditional and object-oriented methodologies.

3.1 Middle-Out Strategy

Increasingly, IT is expected to help firms meet their business challenges by delivering new business-critical applications in a timely manner. Reduced time-to-market, improved customer service, and reduced costs are often critical factors in an organization's success and survival.

The *waterfall approach* suggests that each phase be completed in its entirety before considering subsequent phases without plans or the option to return to earlier, completed phases. The *spiral approach* to systems development is accomplished by iterating through the delivery process, a little analysis, a little design, a little build and test, and back to more analysis. Both typically begin at the top and proceed step-by-step to the bottom.

A delivery process must be more sophisticated than a stepwise navigation of the life cycle. An event-partitioned approach is not a top-down approach in which the system is viewed as a single entity and then successively decomposed until an adequate level of detail is obtained. Event-driven partitions are derived at the middle of the hierarchy with activities that are familiar to the user. They are then synthesized upward to the context diagram and decomposed downward to reach the necessary processing detail. An event-driven approach can be used with a waterfall approach, but, as discussed earlier, the spiral model with iteration and incremental delivery fits the dynamic software environments found today.

3.2   Conceptual Models and the Reduced Role of the DFD

Thinking conceptually (in nonphysical or technology-independent terms) in some phases of the development life cycle and physically in others has its roots in problem-solving theory. It is typically better to isolate one aspect of a problem and explore its solution and then move on to another aspect until all the individual aspects have been solved. Finally, synthesize the partial solutions into a problem solution.

> **Thinking conceptually.** Considering the abstract elements of the problem at hand without considering the physical and technological aspects.

These concepts can be applied to systems design. First, identify and define what the system must do (the logical or conceptual solution) before decisions are made on how the new system will be implemented (the physical solution). This will allow highly focused sessions with the users in order to determine the system's requirements without the constraints that the physical world imposes. After the conceptual solution is defined, the physical solution can be investigated and creative alternative configurations defined as options.

Each event-response partition is loosely coupled to other system partitions and has no direct data flows to any other part of the system. Since coupling occurs only through the stored data, a system Data Flow Diagram (DFD) is not needed. (These diagrams have typically been too big and too complex to be of much value anyway.) The System Response Table (SRT) will serve as the "system model." This reduces the use of the DFD to the modeling of individual subsystems, but does not minimize its importance. Most of the value of the DFD has always been that it reveals and documents hidden functions and provides more understanding of system detail; that role remains.

3.3   Business Events and RAD

"Rapid application development (RAD) is the merger of various structured techniques (especially from data-driven information engineering) with prototyping techniques and joint application development techniques to accelerate systems development" [Whitten and Bentley, 1998]. It combines design, construction, and testing, along with advanced tools, into a single effort and assembles a solution from a combination of existing and newly developed components. But as good as it sounds, the method has a history of developing poorly designed systems and is not considered an effective choice for defining requirements for large systems.

The Gartner Group uses the acronym RAAD (Rapid *Architected* Application Development) to refer to rapid development combined with a sound, scalable software architecture and a defined project structure. "Unfortunately, in real-life projects, we find fitness for business purpose is all too often sacrificed in the rush to meet unrealistic deadlines under the banner of RAD. This is the irresponsible side of RAD: no modeling, uncontrolled RAD based on hacking away in a GUI builder to produce fast results, which are usually unpredictable and difficult to maintain" [Allen and Frost, 1998].

An event-driven approach produces system partitions that have high cohesion and low coupling and can be treated as independent subsystems. They can be designed, coded, and tested individually, and most are candidates for prototyping. Events provide structure in the requirements definition phase that is persistent throughout the delivery process and provides a foundation and a structure for subsequent RAAD.

3.4   Responding to Change

David Taylor, in his book *Object Technology*, discusses the adaptive organization.

> Natural selection, the engine of adaptation in all living systems, has just shifted into high gear. It is now operating at the level of organizations rather than organisms, and the cycle of adaptations is measured in months rather than millennia. The competitive environment of business is continuously changing, and the pace of that change is increasing at an accelerating rate. Where it was once possible for a company to stake out its marketing turf and defend its position for years, static positioning is now viable only in a few isolated industries. For most companies today, the only constant is change. . . . The key to survival in today's chaotic business environment is rapid adaptation. The adaptive organization can move quickly into new market niches, deliver custom solutions instead of fixed products, and continuously outmaneuver its competition in the ongoing battle for market share. [Taylor, 1998]

"Although information systems now allow organizations to do things that would have been unthinkable prior to the advent of computers, there is one thing they hinder far more than help: the process of change" [Taylor, 1998]. Business change is natural and continuous in a world market during a technological era. Since a high percentage of what organizations do is linked to information systems, the system portfolio is also in a state of constant fluctuation. This system change has many implications because it requires significant resources and reduces the resources needed for new development. This in turn can slow an organization's competitive progress and typically commands one of the bigger budgets in the firm. For more about "The adaptive organization," see Chapter 9 of David Taylor's book *Object Technology: A Manager's Guide* [1998].

3.4.1 What Makes Software Change Difficult?

As early as the publication of Tom DeMarco's *Structured Analysis and System Specification,* it was understood that the way that two software units were related affected the potential for the "ripple effect" when one unit was modified—that is, the more coupling between units of software, the more difficult it is to change one without affecting the other. DeMarco stated it like this: "The higher the coupling, the more likely it is that changes to the inside of one module will affect the proper functioning of another module. Obviously coupling is something we would like to minimize" [1979].

Information systems can be composed of millions of lines of code. Many of the business functions that are being simulated have strong relationships to other business components. As the structure of a system is evolving, the coupling between software components can be extensive. It is a key objective of software developers to minimize the strength of component couples, and failing to do so will increase the impact of system modifications. The inherent complexity of information systems along with, in many cases, the added complexity of poor system design makes software change difficult.

3.4.2 Anatomy of System Change

A change in an organization's business can manifest itself in various ways in an information system. For example, each of the following business changes can cause related changes in an information system.

- A federal agency requires a new data element on a report.

- A federal agency changes the rules on how a calculation is made.

- New data is captured by marketing and must be stored in the database.

An examination of system changes reveals the following types. Each of these conditions can be exacerbated if the required new data does not already exist in the input data structure.

- System output to an external agent

- System output to stored data

- System input from an external agent

- System input from stored data

- A processing rule

- A combination of two or more of the above

When it becomes necessary to change an output, one or more of the following modifications will need to be made: addition of a new input data structure, a change in an existing input data structure, a change in the transformation code, and a change in an output data structure. A change in system input will likely require a change in an input data structure, whereas a change in the transformation rules, such as a new algorithm for calculating sales tax, will require a change in the system processing code.

Many times business change makes it necessary to produce new system capabilities that require response to a new business event. If the stored data supports the new functionality, designing and coding a new event response is straightforward and takes on the nature of a new project. If the current stored data will not support the added functionality, database change can be necessary and may present a much larger problem.

Modification of production systems also involves change testing, regression testing, documentation updates, and the scheduling of placement of the modified code back into an operational status.

3.4.3 Changes in Event Responses

A business event is, by its very nature, some activity in the business, and a change in the business will likely be reflected in an associated information subsystem. When an event response in the system changes, the impact of the change will vary between an event-partitioned system and an object-partitioned system.

When an event-partitioned scheme is followed, the impact of a change in a business event will be isolated to a single, conceptual unit of processing. Even though the response is likely to be made up of many components, they are all identified as belonging to the event response undergoing change.

When an object-partitioned approach is used, the change in a single business event and its associated response will be dispersed among the collaborating object classes. This may involve class methods and/or class data. In some cases, it may also require changes in one or more method interfaces.

Owing to the independence of event-partitioned responses, a new event response can be added without affecting existing parts of the system. Similarly, a new class can be added when object partitioning is used, and because of the power of polymorphism, existing code may not require modification.

3.4.4 Adaptive Systems

Systems must be designed to be as adaptive as possible to support the dynamic, competitive nature of today's organizations. Modularization with high cohesion and low coupling and with well-defined, simple interfaces to encapsulate both private data and processing tends to isolate changes to individual processing units. The ripple effect is minimized. Designing partitions of the system to represent well-defined business functions also helps to associate business changes with units of the system and to minimize the number of components involved. Low coupling and high cohesion with units of the system defined by their interfaces are no longer just "desirable" properties; they have become a necessity from the top of the system structure to the bottom.

By their nature, event partitions align software components closely with the business functions. Since the data tends to be more stable than the processing, most changes are in business function and consequently in processing components of the system. Business change can often be associated with a single event response, and modification of the system can often be isolated to that single response. Because event responses are persistent from the top to the bottom of the life cycle, changes in business function are more easily tracked to the target system components.

On the object side, polymorphism offers a way to reduce the number of software units involved in a particular change [Taylor, 1998], but reuse through inheritance comes with a price. Inheritance disperses the properties of a class across the class hierarchy, forcing the consideration of many classes outside the scope of the business change.

It is imperative that systems be responsive to change. Businesses cannot be competitive if their information systems cannot keep pace with the business.

Plans can be severely constrained and market share lost if an organization's vision cannot be accomplished because the software cannot meet future demands quickly.

3.5   Adopting an Event-Driven Approach for Your Organization

The impact of making a major paradigm switch in a corporate software environment is well known. It is typically brutal. There is an instant loss of production for those involved in the new approach, and the normal work routine is disrupted for a significant amount of time.

Training takes resources away from the tasks of maintenance and new development, and the cost of instructors is very high. After training is complete, productivity is impacted by the learning curve of the new methods as well as by a lack of experienced personnel to assist with problems. Yet another area of concern can be support tools. The initial cost of these tools and the time and resources required to implement, support, and learn to use them add to the expense of conversion.

Adopting an event-driven approach to the delivery process is probably as painless as could be expected. Events happen in the user's domain. Consequently, these new ideas will likely be accepted by the users with heartfelt gratitude since a project begins on their turf; it is their system, and their expectations must be met.

Even though partitioning requirements around events may represent a significant change in the requirements gathering effort, downstream phases will benefit rather than suffer from the partitioning scheme and will experience little impact. The partitions of the system will be more intuitive and real-world, and communication with the users will be easier to maintain. The disruption will be isolated to the early phase of the delivery process. However, if the Information Systems (IS) group is not currently following a set of formal, consistent methods for requirements definition, benefits will be realized in this early phase as well as a result of the discipline that is added to the process.

It is recommended that an organization consider the following approach when changing to an event-driven strategy.

- Train a small team in the new methods.

- Implement the new approach for a small, pilot project that is not mission-critical.

- Allow time for the capture of metrics to be used for assessment of future projects and for comparison with past development efforts.

- Get some outside help on this first project.

- Document the advantages and disadvantages that are experienced throughout the delivery process.

Any organization that has gone through significant change knows the impact that it can have. When switching to something as natural and intuitive as using business events as the primary partitioning strategy for their information systems, the transition is often relatively easy.

3.5.1 Tailoring Methods

The models and techniques shown in this guide have worked well for me and for many other information system analysts. Most engineering disciplines build models before they build the final product, and diagrams, tables, and pseudocode work well for modeling software requirements. In contrast, the English language is not known as an effective medium for technical specification.

To keep this guide concise and to the point, only one model type or technique has been presented for each system artifact—but there are other ways to represent the various components of a proposed system. For example, functional structure can be represented with a diagram or with an outline, as shown in Figure 3.1. Diagrams are typically more easily analyzed and verified, while an outline is more easily maintained.

Table columns can be altered to vary the information captured, and many different formats can be used to describe business procedures. Clarity of process steps and verification are important considerations when business scenarios are

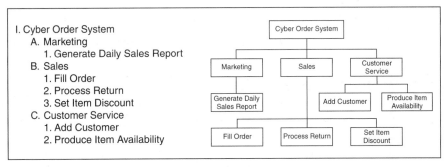

Figure 3.1   System functional structure

being described. There are also variations in notation for many of the diagrams used in this book, and each has its own advantages and disadvantages. My own favorites have typically been used—for example, the "crow's foot" for entity relationships and Gane-Sarson for DFDs. Yourdon notation could be used just as effectively.

Finally, I like a structured English pseudocode for representing logic. It is easy to create, maintain, and verify and can easily be tailored to each organization. Other techniques of representing logic, such as Action Diagrams, could be used. Some organizations describe the response to an event using the English language. My experience has shown that specifications represented in English text are difficult to analyze, verify, and maintain.

Although these models can be developed by hand, it is terribly inefficient and maintenance is a nightmare. Available tools vary in cost from a few thousand dollars to six figures and offer a variety of functionality. While a very inexpensive tool might suffice for a small pilot study, the midrange tools offer both adequate functionality and relative ease of use and as a minimum are required for most corporate projects. These tools will likely be used for extensive peer reviews and will often involve subject-matter expert verification.

My own most recent experience was with System Architect by Popkin Software and Systems, Inc. It performed well and offers support for both traditional and object-oriented approaches. It is recommended that a tool provide at least the following.

- A repository that links the components of different models such as an entity from the Entity Relationship Diagram (ERD) to the corresponding data store in a DFD

- Support for both object-oriented and traditional methods

- Unified Modeling Language (UML) support

- Robust textual support at a level below, but linked to, the diagrams

3.6   Methodology Overview

A diagrammatic overview of the requirements definition process *(Requirements Delivery Process Map)* is included at the end of this section (see Figure 3.2). A brief discussion of each of the map components follows. Using joint sessions, the team begins by documenting and modeling two aspects of the system: the responses to the business events that are relevant to the system under study (Behavior Model) and the data that will be needed to support system processing (Data Model). The event list partitions the system into independent responses to activities that are carried out in the user environment. As the data model is developed, business rules that govern the capture and transformation of data are discovered.

Between these two analysis activities, the team very quickly (in a week to a few weeks) brings the users on-board and documents many important high-level system characteristics. Users and developers alike see progress very early in the project life cycle. Other components of the behavior model (context diagram, scenarios, decomposition diagram, and system response table) can be developed as needed to enhance the understanding and documentation of the system.

Project outcome can typically be improved if the analysis team models each business event using an event diagram (Process Model). The models are not difficult to build, and they force an increasing understanding of the way in which each event response uses data and interacts with the user. The depth to which these models are subsequently taken depends on budget and schedule considerations as well as the team's confidence in their value and the team's understanding of the complex processing algorithms of the proposed system. The event diagrams are very useful for the subsequent prototyping of the user interfaces and the simpler database accesses. Regardless of the methods chosen, the objective is to document, as a response to a business event, the user interface (both input and output), the business rules for the transformation of the data, the required stored data, and the interface to the stored data.

What the system must do to respond to the external environment is now understood, and in an event-oriented methodology only the interaction between the data and the processing components remains to be studied (Interaction Model). But in an object-oriented approach, much remains to be done. Object classes must be assembled by examining the way in which each data entity from the ERD is used by the functions and subfunctions identified in the event diagrams. An additional diagram is then needed to show how these object classes collaborate to respond to each business event.

Another analysis activity that can be very time-effective and cost-effective is development of the interaction model. Examination of the system from the perspective of the interaction between the data and the system responses gives us yet another aspect of the system. Because an omission in the analysis phase becomes much more expensive when discovered in later phases, this activity can be very valuable by revealing the omission of system data or required processes.

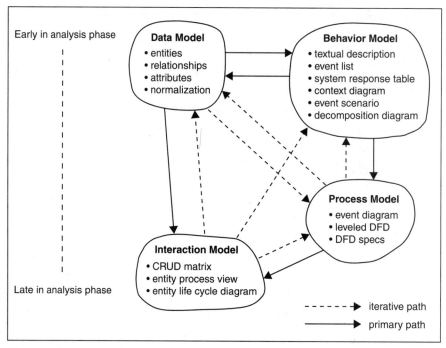

Figure 3.2   Requirements delivery process map

PART II

Event-Partitioned
System Requirements

Part II presents a toolbox of techniques and methods for requirements analysis and specification that are event-driven at both the user interface and the system-partitioning levels. Business events are documented early in the requirements phase and drive the partitioning of the system throughout the delivery process. Not only are business events used to drive the user interface, but they also partition the system into very independent subsystems, each having the responsibility of responding to a single business event.

The methods presented here are most effective when used in a repetitive fashion, moving like a pinball back and forth among the models that bring the most value to the project (toolbox approach). Although the methods have some dependencies, they are used *iteratively* and in parallel, and some may not be used at all. No order of use is implied by the order of presentation in each chapter. The spiral model of the delivery process is a common way to implement iteration, and, when used along with "proof of concept" prototyping, Joint Application Workshops (JAWs), and an incremental delivery approach, can accelerate the system requirements definition effort.

The approach presented also investigates the proposed system from multiple aspects. System behavior, system data, and system processing are all examined iteratively to provide the greater understanding of each perspective that occurs as we revisit models in a spiral of learning and insight.

This part of the guide begins with system behavior and then follows with system data models, process models, and interaction models. In practice, it is recommended that the system behavior and system data be considered simultaneously since each contributes to the other. Many of the methods shown for event partitioning can be reused for the object partitioning discussion in Part IV. The final chapter discusses the transition from the conceptual models to a physical design. Each chapter subsection discusses a technique and then presents the technique, an example, and associated tips. A collection of the examples that appear in Chapters 5 through 9 is available in

Appendix A for examination and comparison, and a key to the symbols used in the diagrams can be found in Appendix B. Additional discussion of many of the methods presented in Chapters 4 through 9 can be found in *Yourdon Systems Method* [Yourdon, 1993] and *Systems Analysis and Design Methods* [Whitten and Bentley, 1998].

CHAPTER FOUR

Project Procedure for Event Partitioning

- ■ **4.1 System Behavior**
- ■ **4.2 System Data**
- ■ **4.3 System Process**
- ■ **4.4 Data/Process Interaction**
- ■ **4.5 Transition to Physical Design**
- ■ **4.6 Event-Partitioned Deliverables**

Issues such as schedule and budget will require some effort at the beginning of a project but for the most part will be considered only in this chapter. This book also assumes that system feasibility has been considered and that it has been agreed to begin development. The task of defining system requirements is one of thoroughly understanding the proposed system and documenting the "essence" of that system—that is, those requirements that a system must satisfy in order to fulfill its purpose, regardless of how the system is implemented. Each of the artifacts discussed in this chapter will be developed in detail in Chapters 5 to 9.

To begin requirements definition, schedule a meeting to establish an upper-level view of the system to start everyone down the same path. This meeting is a good time to stress the necessity of *the user group taking responsibility for system content*. Make a strong argument that it is the users' system and not the developers' system. At this time, establish the need for participation of users in subsequent joint sessions and establish approximate time requirements for these sessions. From

20 to 30 hours for the first month of requirements definition for key users is not unusual but will pay off in the long run with reduced delivery time and a higher-quality system. Explain that participation in joint sessions is vital if system development is to be accelerated and is to meet the users' expectations.

For managing the remainder of the system development effort, let the deliverables drive the team's procedure, being careful not to fall into the trap of a step-by-step, waterfall methodology. Although some deliverables are clearly dependent on others, they should be developed in parallel when possible. Some teams have been observed skipping some of them when the schedule was particularly tight. Just keep in mind that as deliverables are dropped, the risk of omitting requirements rises.

Also, an "accelerated development" mindset must be had by all. If the typical Structured Development Life Cycle (SDLC) methodology has been used in the past, now think in terms of speeding things up. Believe that there is a faster and better way of doing the system analysis and design. Quality is not being compromised—it cannot be. But business events, strong data modeling, Joint Application Workshops (JAWs), and prototyping will be used to accelerate the requirements definition, and the user will be involved as a team member, not just as an external entity. If the period of time across which definition occurs is shortened, the business changes less (remains more stable) and therefore requirements better match the business being modeled.

The following deliverables (business event list, business event scenarios, etc.) can be used as a checklist and as a basis for project management. The reader's attention is directed to Figure 3.2 for a map of the requirements delivery process.

4.1 System Behavior

Following the first iteration of documenting system purpose, objectives, critical success factors, and constraints, the analysis team begins to define the way in which the system will behave. The system behavior model defines and documents how the system will respond to the user (but not the processing details).

The behavior model treats each system response to a business event as a black box—that is, it defines the response but not the internal processing necessary to generate that response.

4.1.1 Business Event List

Using JAWs, begin developing the business event list. This list is developed in the users' language, and the users will typically drive the effort. In a separate list, document all business events that are discussed but turn out to be out of the proposed system scope. This will add definition to the nonobjectives listed in the system charter.

> As the team begins to bog down in the behavior effort, move to the data. When both models seem fairly stable, move to the next set of activities, knowing that these models will be revisited as the project proceeds.

4.1.2 Business Event Scenarios

Have the user groups develop a scenario for each event identified in the event list. These scenarios should define the sequence of activities that make up use of the system when each event is experienced and define the system response to each event. Some scenarios may include more than one event.

Using joint development sessions, review the scenarios and tie down the anticipated response of the proposed system to the events in the event list. If the users cannot do this because they do not have time or because they are not sure what they want, the odds of delivering an effective system on schedule are slim at this point in time.

4.1.3 System Response Table

The team can now develop a System Response Table (SRT). This will define the expected system response to the business events and will set software scope for the first time in the project. There is one row in the table for each business event. This is one of the most important activities of the entire project since it partitions the proposed system on the basis of the user's view of the system. These partitions have low coupling and can be approached as subsystems to be developed and tested separately from other partitions. They can then be clustered into applications for phased releases as schedule and resources permit or dictate.

4.1.4 Context Diagram

A context diagram can now be developed that represents diagrammatically the information in the SRT. It is a Data Flow Diagram (DFD) that shows all external agents and their input and output interfaces to the system. The process is a "black box" having the system name.

4.1.5 Decomposition Diagram

Develop a decomposition diagram with the business area's functional areas represented near the top levels. For each row in the SRT, add a process at the bottom level of the diagram associated with the functional area having responsibility for that process. This can facilitate setting up joint development sessions or pursuing joint session follow-up by indicating those responsible for each event response.

4.2 System Data

Following the first iteration of the system charter, the analysis team begins to define the data requirements along with the way in which the system will behave. The data model identifies and documents entities about which data must be stored and how the data entities relate to each other.

> The data is documented in an Entity Relationship Diagram (ERD) and includes data entities, data entity relationships, data entity attributes, and data entity attribute definitions (data type, length, null requirements, domain, and default value).

4.2.1 Entity Relationship Diagram

In parallel to some extent, begin developing the ERD. This actually should be started after the initial business event list is developed but should not wait until the event list is finished. These two efforts support each other and work on one typically reveals much about the other. The same people should participate in both by alternating back and forth between the two models. If schedule and budget permit, extend the scope of the data model beyond the scope of the system under study to include the entire business area (marketing, for example).

> As the team begins to bog down in the data requirements effort, move back to system behavior. When both models seem fairly stable, move to the next set of activities knowing that these models will be revisited as the project proceeds.

4.3 System Process

It is now time to document the details of the processing necessary to respond to each business event included in the scope of the system. Using DFDs, the required data and the data transformation rules for each business event response will be defined and documented.

4.3.1 Event Diagram

For each row in the SRT (each event response), develop an event DFD. This will document the inputs and outputs from external agents and from the stored data components. Each event response is only a black box at this time. Processing logic will be documented later.

4.3.2 Leveled DFD

For any event response for which understanding is lacking or that contains significant complexity, develop a leveled DFD. Generally, event partitioning derives relatively small subsystems and one level of decomposition is sufficient. When needed, however, this will further partition the complexity and reveal necessary processing as well as promote understanding of data usage and requirements. Many interfaces with the database are common enough that leveling below the event diagrams is neither necessary nor profitable.

4.3.3 DFD Specification

Using structured English, define the logic for each bottom-level process in the DFDs. Also, define the attributes for each data flow on the event diagrams. This documentation is somewhat time-consuming, but errors or omissions are much less expensive to fix if discovered now rather than later, and the effort promotes understanding.

4.3.4 Prototype

Prototype the event responses that have user interfaces and/or simple database accesses. This requires a fourth-generation language and produces a software component that will either evolve throughout the development life cycle or be disposed of after the design phase. If the event response has a component that should be implemented as a stored procedure rather than as part of the interface software, it can be stubbed and developed later.

4.4 Data/Process Interaction

Data has little value until it is transformed into an output product. As time and resources permit and as necessary, develop interaction models to validate the interaction between the processing necessary for this transformation and the required data for each output product. Choose the ones that offer the most value for the project. Of the interaction techniques discussed here, the CRUD matrix typically yields the best return on investment.

4.4.1 CRUD Matrix

Examine the event diagrams and develop a CRUD (Create, Read, Update, Delete) matrix. This technique provides a means of examining the interaction between data entities in the data model and the event responses by documenting for which of the four functions each event response is responsible.

4.4.2 Entity Process View

For each event diagram, develop an Entity Process View (EPV). This technique will allow and encourage the development team to focus on the data and data relationships as they relate to the processes for each event response. Required relationships often are indicative of required processing, and one-to-many relationships frequently reveal iterative processing needs.

4.4.3 Entity Life Cycle Diagram

Develop an Entity Life Cycle Diagram (ELCD) for each entity having a rich life cycle. A data entity life cycle can be examined by the team by listing its states. If the states are rich and reveal significant information about the events of the system, diagram the entity life cycle and compare it with the system specifications for completeness.

4.5   Transition to Physical Design

When the system analysis identifies and defines a large number of events to which the system must respond, the proposed system should be partitioned into multiple applications or releases. This will allow development to be scheduled into projects a few months in length. The transition to design documents this project content based on system priorities and data dependence.

The event responses have low coupling characteristics and are very independent. They can be developed and tested individually, simplifying project management. This partitioning scheme provides excellent traceability back to the original business events defined by the users since the event constructs defined in analysis are persistent through design and construction.

4.5.1   System Releases

Document system priorities and determine an order of development of the system partitions (event responses) by defining incremental system releases. Some of the event responses will typically have higher priorities than will others, but this is not the only factor that must be considered. While event-partitioned systems have fairly low coupling, they still can have strong data dependencies, and these must take precedence over business needs to preserve data integrity. System release information can be documented in the SRT.

4.5.2   System Distribution

Document a view of how the users of the proposed system will be distributed. Develop a matrix of event responses and user locations, identifying which responses are needed at each location. Using the CRUD matrix, develop a second distribution matrix that documents which data entities are required at each location and how each entity will be used (C, R, U, or D).

4.6   Event-Partitioned Deliverables

The *deliverables* of a methodology are the products (lists, diagrams, and descriptions) that are generated to document the requirements and specifications of an information system. These products are presented in Tables 4.1 through 4.5.

Table 4.1.   Behavior Model Deliverables

Deliverable	Responsibility
JAD schedule and attendance list	Project leader
Business event list	Analyst
Business event scenarios	Project leader*
System response table	Analyst
Textual description of each business event response	Analyst
Context diagram	Analyst
Decomposition diagram	Analyst

*Completed by user group.
Because a "toolbox" approach is used, some deliverables may be omitted on the basis of project needs.

Table 4.2.   Data Model Deliverables

Deliverable	Responsibility
Entity Relationship Diagram	Analyst
Relationship diagram	
Attributes	
Attribute definition	

Table 4.3.   Process Model Deliverables

Deliverable	Responsibility
Event DFDs	Analyst
Leveled DFDs	Analyst
Process specifications	Analyst
Data flow definitions	Analyst

Leveled DFDs may not provide value for most event responses.

Table 4.4.   Interaction Model Deliverables

Deliverable	Responsibility
CRUD matrix	Analyst
Entity process views	Analyst
Entity life cycle diagrams	Analyst

Some development teams will choose to omit some of these deliverables.

Table 4.5.   Transition to Design Deliverables

Deliverable	Responsibility
System releases	Analyst
Event geography table	Analyst
Data geography table	Analyst

One or more of these deliverables may be omitted.

CHAPTER FIVE

System Behavior

- **5.1 Business Event**
- **5.2 System Response**
- **5.3 System Context**
- **5.4 Business Event Scenario**
- **5.5 Functional Structure**

As a development team begins to explore the processing requirements of a proposed system, it is important to define the way in which the system will respond to the user. The users of the system, the business events to which the system will respond, the inputs that will trigger the response, and the outputs generated by the system make up the system behavior. System behavior is viewed from multiple perspectives in the following models. The components of the behavior model are described in this chapter and are shown here in the context of the entire methodology.

Business event
System response
System context
Business event scenario
Functional structure

Event response
Process decomposition
Event-response specification

Data entity
Entity relationship
Entity attribute
Data normalization

CRUD associations
Entity process view
Entity life cycle
System releases
System distribution

5.1   Business Event

The event list establishes the scope of the system in terms of the business area activities that will be involved with the system. It documents the events in the business area to which the proposed system is obligated to respond and involves the user group early in the analysis effort.

Each business event identifies the business role that will initiate contact with the system, the action taking place in the business area, and an abstract representation of the trigger that will invoke a system response. Events are described in the language of the business area. There are two types of events: external and temporal. An external event happens in the business area and sends a trigger to invoke a dedicated part of the system (events 1–5 in the example in Section 5.1.2). A temporal event activates a system response when a point in time is reached (event 6 in the example) or when a defined time interval has passed.

These business events begin to partition the proposed system at the most abstract level. A part of the system will be dedicated to support each business activity defined by an event and will be specified in more detail in subsequent models.

5.1.1 Technique

- In a joint design session, the user group is asked to identify which business activities need to be supported by the proposed system. To get things going, the analysis team can have a few in mind from their review of the system objectives and the current business activities.

- Document these activities in the normalized form subject/verb/object (see the example below), where the subject is the business role interfacing with the system and the object is the trigger (the input that will activate the system).

- Add a separate textual description for each event if additional information is necessary for a full understanding of the business activity, keeping in mind that a scenario can be generated if desired.

5.1.2 Example

Some of the events listed below are not supported by the abbreviated data model.

1. Customer places order
2. Customer returns item
3. Person requests customer status
4. Management submits item discount information
5. Customer inquires about item availability
6. Time to generate daily sales report

5.1.3 Risk if Not Completed

When the analysis methodology follows an event-driven approach as outlined in this book, the event list must be completed. It is the basis for user participation and is the foundation for subsequent models; the entire methodology is dependent on it.

5.1.4 Technique Tips

- Use the language of the business area when describing events.

- Make sure that the user understands that, at a high level, the scope of the system is being established by the event list and that it must be a thorough effort.

- Scenarios will be used to describe in more detail each event and the subsequent interface with the system including the expected system response.

- Temporal events are typically documented as "Time to 'verb/object'" (see event 6).

- Ask the users to describe anything that occurs in their work areas that might involve the proposed system.

Project Management Tips—Business Event List

- Make your case with user management that you must have user time for Joint Application Workshops (JAWs). These sessions will pay back many times over as development moves to the later phases of the life cycle. They are vital to identifying requirements and setting scope.
- The project leader can begin to control "scope creep" early in the life cycle by emphasizing that this activity sets system scope at a high level.
- This will be the first contact with most of the users. Be sure to emphasize that business events are from their domain, are from their perspective, and are to be described in their business language. This is a chance to bring the user group on-board early in the project life cycle.
- For the joint sessions, publish a detailed schedule of topics so users can attend when the topics are relevant.
- "Time box" the joint sessions so they can be attended appropriately and so the sessions will not bog down. Additional sessions may have to be scheduled to deal with unresolved issues.
- The project leader may not want to be the facilitator of the joint sessions. He or she may need to be free during the sessions to look for trouble spots and lead the group to resolution.
- Scenarios may also work here if the user has difficulty zeroing in on single business events. The events can be factored out later.

5.2   System Response

The System Response Table (SRT) documents an abstraction of the processing that will take place when each trigger is received by the system. It is a collection of system responses to the business events in the event list.

The SRT names the system response to each event. It also documents the source of each trigger, the trigger (system input), the major system outputs, and the destinations of the outputs.

Each event response (each row in the table in Section 5.2.2) is the root of the subsequent model fragments that will be developed. Each partition of the system that is represented by a row in the table will be modeled using Data Flow Diagrams (DFDs), entity process views, and a CRUD matrix.

Business event
▶ **System response**
System context
Business event scenario
Functional structure

5.2.1 Technique

- A partition of the system will be dedicated to responding to each business event. Establish a row in the SRT and name a response to each event in the event list. Use the verb/object form for each event response. For example, the system will "Fill order" in response to the event "Customer places order."

- For each event response, identify the source of the trigger. It should be a role in the business area and not a specific person or thing. It has likely been identified in the event list.

- Name each trigger. The name should be a noun or adjective/noun and should represent the input that invokes a system response.

- Document the major outputs that will be generated by each event response. Include those that are put to data stores.

- Name the destination of each output.

- It can be valuable to expand the first column (E1, for example) to allow for the normalized form of each business event.

5.2.2 Example

Table 5.1.   Cyber Order System—System Response Table

Event	Source	Trigger	Event Response	Major Output	External Destination
E1	Customer	Order	Fill order	• Invoice • Order • Inventory update • Pick list	• Customer • Warehouse • Database
E2	Customer	Item	Process return	• Inventory update • Damaged item list	• Database • Management
E3	Candidate customer	Customer status request	Add customer	• New customer	• Database
E4	Management	Discount information	Record discount information	• Validated discount information	• Database
E5	Customer	Item availability request	Produce item availability	• Item availability	• Customer
E6		(Temporal)	Generate daily sales report	• Daily sales report	• Sales department

A variation of this table may be preferable for some development teams. For example, some teams omit the last two columns.

5.2.3 Risk if Not Completed

When the analysis methodology follows an event-driven approach as outlined in this book, this table is the only documentation of the collection of system response partitions.

5.2.4 Technique Tips

- Only one trigger can activate an event response (by definition of an event, Chapter 1), but more than one external agent can be the source of a particular trigger. If more than one trigger is involved, then more than one event is involved.

- Many of the outputs generated by a system are directed to the eventual database. It is not valuable at this time to name a specific data entity, since this will be modeled in the event DFDs.

- The Context Diagram (described in the next section) will represent this table diagrammatically.

- A system partition must be able to provide all of the required processing when the trigger is received and return to an idle state awaiting another instance of the event trigger.

- An event can send only one trigger to the system. If another trigger appears to invoke the same partition, two event responses have been combined and must be separated.

- Many custodial functions (update and delete) are not identified as business events and are therefore often not modeled. Custodial functions are

---

Project Management Tips—System Response Table

- This is the first attempt to identify the business event triggers and how the system will respond to those triggers. This is best elicited from the user, but it is suggested that it be a separate effort from identification of business events.
- Make it clear that the users are defining system scope with this effort by defining the triggers to which the system will respond and the products that will be generated by the system.
- This will be the project leader's "whole view" of the system. Each row of the table is a system partition that will persist throughout the system development effort. Because of its low coupling with other partitions, an event response can be developed as an individual subsystem.

required to maintain the stored data, and it is understood that they will be developed.

- List only major output products, enough to define what this event response produces.

5.3   System Context

The Context Diagram can be used to motivate (encourage) dialogue early in the requirements definition effort and to capture a high-level view of the system interfaces.

This is a DFD with a single process representing the entire system along with the major interfaces of the system. Sources of data and receivers of system output (external agents), along with the inputs and outputs or composite inputs and outputs of the system, are shown.

The Context Diagram (Figure 5.1) represents all of the event responses in the event table and thus all of the processes in the system. The external agents and system inputs and outputs are also shown in the event table but are represented diagrammatically in this model. The input and output flows will be shown in more detail in event response DFDs while data flow attributes are defined in the Entity Relationship Diagram (ERD).

5.3.1 Technique

- Begin with a "first-cut" model developed by the IS team followed by user joint sessions to complete. This is a DFD, so follow the appropriate DFD rules (see Technique Tips under Event Response in Chapter 7).

- Create a process representing the total system under study.

- Identify the major inputs that originate outside the system and to which the system must respond (be sensitive to).

- Identify the source of each input.

- Add these external agents and input flows to the diagram.

- Identify the output items the system will produce in response to the inputs.

- Identify the receivers of the outputs.

- Add these external agents and output flows to the diagram.

- Add external databases to which the system will interface (*Purchasing* in the example).

5.3.2 Example

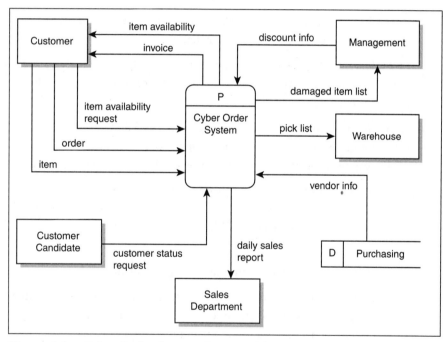

Figure 5.1   Cyber Order System Context Diagram

5.3.3 Risk if Not Completed

The Context Diagram presents an overview of the proposed system and helps identify user groups with which the IS team must interact. Although everything shown here will be shown elsewhere, not developing this diagram will preclude the opportunity for a focal point for some early high-level discussion that can be very valuable. It requires little time to construct if done in parallel with, or following, the event table.

5.3.4 Technique Tips

- Scope is much more fully defined by the event table and subsequent event-response detail.

- Don't spend too much time on this diagram by itself, because much more understanding of the system interfaces will be gained during event analysis.

- Even though iteration is very important, don't iterate through this diagram too often. After a "first-cut" pass, wait to complete it after event analysis, if possible.

- To keep the diagram readable, show composite data flows when the inputs and outputs begin to crowd the diagram.

- Develop the Context Diagram in parallel with event analysis, because much of what is discovered during development of this diagram can be captured in the event table.

- When defining external agents, keep in mind that a role that is outside of the system is being defined even though that object may also have a system role (example: customer is an external agent and also a data entity in the database).

- Medium-to-large systems have too many inputs and outputs to show individually; composite flows must be used for these systems, which in turn often reduce the diagram's value.

- This diagram represents scope but certainly does not define it. At best, it defines the scope of the interfaces with the business area.

- Some methodologies do not represent external databases on the Context Diagram while others do, since it may reveal and document a very complex system interface (see Purchasing in the example).

- Do not show the database of the system being modeled, since it is represented within the system process.

- Some methodologies encourage duplication of terminators to avoid unnecessary clutter.

- Use the SRT as the source for the components of this diagram (external agent, trigger, generated product, product destination).

> ### Project Management Tips—Context Diagram
>
> - Some teams do not develop the Context Diagram because it can become very cluttered or highly composite. As project leader, know how you will use it before consuming resources to build it.
> - Some users relate to a diagram better than to the SRT. This is the primary reason to develop the Context Diagram.
> - One person can typically handle the responsibility for developing and maintaining this diagram.
> - Don't spend too much time on this diagram by itself, because much more understanding of the system interfaces will be gained during event analysis (the business event list and SRT).
> - Use early in the requirements analysis phase, in parallel with event analysis.

5.4 Business Event Scenario

Business event scenarios encourage the user group, early in the requirements definition effort, to get serious about how they expect to interface with the proposed system and what system response they expect to get.

Development of event scenarios is primarily the responsibility of the user group. They take on a business area perspective and are descriptions of system interfaces and of system expectations. A scenario is a step-by-step description of what happens in the business area that motivates the user to seek support from the system, how the system will be invoked, and what the system must produce.

Event scenarios describe business events in more detail than the normalized form used in the event list. They are useful as inputs to the development of the SRT and also as references for acceptance testing.

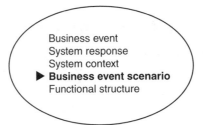

5.4.1 Technique

This is a user group effort with technical support given by the analyst.

- Describe the business event that motivates system use.

- Describe step by step how the system user will interface with the system to provide needed data.

- Describe what the system response will be and any special processing that will be needed to generate the output.

5.4.2 Example

An order clerk receives an order from the customer and must collect the required information. The data making up the order is entered into and validated by the computer system. The clerk must be notified of any invalid data and have the option of correcting that data immediately. The system must also check the on-hand quantity of any item ordered and advise the clerk if the amount ordered is not available. An option to partial fill and back order is required when an insufficient quantity exists. When an order is completed, the system should have produced the following.

- Updated inventory counts

- A customer invoice

- A pick list for the warehouse

- A packing slip for the warehouse

5.4.3 Risk if Not Completed

Early, committed, detailed involvement of the user group is vital to system development success and system usability. Event scenarios are only one way of accomplishing this, but the absence of user buy-in and serious involvement can doom a mission-critical project.

5.4.4 Technique Tips

- Analysis is a logical, conceptual effort rather than a physical one, but the users will often find it easier to describe their businesses physically. The users must be comfortable with the final scenarios; the analyst can later derive a nonphysical account of system functionality.

- Scenarios can be developed along with the business events if the users have difficulty identifying single business events.

Project Management Tips–Business Event Scenarios

- Control of user expectations is vital if the final system is to satisfy the user group. Scenarios define what the user *expects* the system to do in response to the business events.
- Scenarios can be used to motivate the users to focus on what the system must do for them.
- Development of scenarios is primarily the responsibility of the user group.
- Plan to use the scenarios in development of the user acceptance tests (UATs).
- Plan a joint session presentation of event scenarios by the user group. Invite high-level management representatives to ensure commitment by those who can make or break a project with their decisions.

5.5 Functional Structure

The Decomposition Diagram (Figure 5.2) allows refinement of the business area functional structure and helps the analyst relate issues about the proposed system to the functional area of the business having responsibility for them. It identifies groups of subsystems that can be used to plan for independent design and implementation. For acceptance testing, it provides one means of tracing the delivered system functionality back to the requesting group. This diagram also can be augmented with names and used to set up joint sessions or follow-up interviews.

The Decomposition Diagram is a hierarchy chart that reveals and documents the hierarchical relationship between functional areas of the business and the functions of the proposed system. It identifies the functional areas of the business and defines the relationship between these functional areas and the event-response subsystems as they are developed.

No other diagram derives directly from this diagram. Since the methods in this handbook follow a middle-out approach, the Decomposition Diagram acts as an integrating mechanism between the high-level representations of the system (such as the Context Diagram) and the middle-level system event responses. Some Computer Aided Software Engineering (CASE) tools require this diagram.

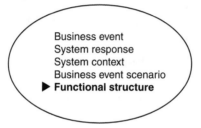

5.5.1 Technique

- Represent the entire system as a single rectangle at the top of the hierarchy.

- Identify functional areas of the business area under study and add them to the diagram as the second level.

- When the number of functional areas is large, a layer can be added between the functional areas and the top of the diagram to generalize or to group functional areas.

- As the system is subsequently partitioned into event responses, add them to the bottom level of the diagram linked to the functional area having responsibility.

5.5.2 Example

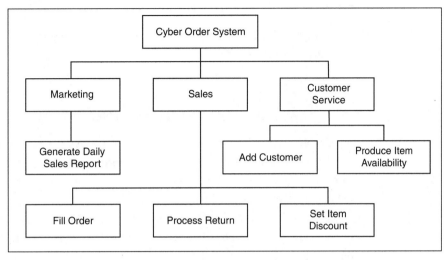

Figure 5.2   Cyber Order System Decomposition Diagram

5.5.3 Risk if Not Completed

Functional relationships within the business area and within the proposed system could be missed or misunderstood or could take longer to identify if not developed as a separate effort. Interfaces with the various user groups may not be as effective if system issues are not always discussed with the most appropriate user. Also, if a phased delivery is planned, important relationships between system functionality and the business area functionality may not be fully understood.

5.5.4 Technique Tips

- Decomposition should not relate to organization structure but instead should be functional in nature.

- Functions often end in "ing," "ance," "ment," or "tion" and are often named with a noun or gerund.

- A Decomposition Diagram represents a "whole-part" hierarchy in which the sum of the functionality of the children equals the parent functionality.

- Functional decomposition is the process of breaking functions into smaller, more descriptive components.

- Functional decomposition is largely an intuitive partitioning technique, not a precise one with a single correct outcome.

- The Decomposition Diagram provides a basis for the higher levels of the menu structure of the system.

Project Management Tips—Decomposition Diagram

- The Decomposition Diagram can help associate system functionality with the user group responsible for it. Therefore, it can help the project leader relate issues about the proposed system to the functional area of the business having responsibility for them.
- Use this diagram to set up joint sessions when subsets of the user group must be scheduled because the user group is too large to invite all at once.
- This diagram can be useful for user acceptance testing (UAT) by associating functionality with test case responsibility. It provides one means of traceability of the delivered system functionality back to the requesting group.
- If a phased delivery is planned, important relationships between system functionality and the business area functionality may be revealed by this diagram.

System Data

> Conceptual database design revolves around discovering and analyzing organizational and user data requirements. This includes identifying what data is important and what data should be maintained. . . . Conceptual models help users and systems developers identify data requirements. Conceptual models are by design abstract. As such, they encourage high-level problem structuring and help establish a common ground on which users and developers can communicate to one another about systems functions. [Sanders, 1995]

Then, by the very nature of system development, the data models are tested as the process models are built and can be modified much more cheaply than physical artifacts later in the development cycle.

The data is modeled to identify those entities and data attributes that must be stored to support a business area's information systems. This model will also document relevant relationships between the data entities that often indicate necessary system behavior and processing. Typically, this model will be implemented as a database.

Information Engineering (IE) is a data-centered, process-sensitive methodology, first proposed by James Martin, that emphasizes the modeling of business areas or enterprise data. If an IE methodology is followed, data for an entire business area will be modeled. This increases the chance that the data will integrate across systems and applications, which implies developing the data model at the beginning of the first project for a business area and then just using, enhancing, and verifying it for subsequent projects. The amount of change that is required for each project depends on the thoroughness of the original modeling effort. It is clear that normalized, modeled data integrates more easily than data without a normalized model.

A data model is built in a "pinball" fashion—that is, the developer bounces around from the entities to the attributes to the relationships, all the time applying normalization rules. The order of presentation of the following topics does not imply development order. There are, however, some dependencies that are intrinsic, such as the need for entities in order to find relationships and the need to find attributes before normalization can take place. For the experienced analyst, normalization seldom moves attributes from one entity to another. Instead, the attributes are placed in the correct entity in the first place, based on the rules of normalization. For the sake of discussion in this chapter, some data may be shown unnormalized in the early stages of the model.

Foreign keys will be shown in this guide even though they represent a possible physical implementation. It is felt that foreign keys, when shown at the conceptual level, can act as an adjunct to defining the relationship for those less experienced in data modeling and database development.

The Entity Relationship Diagram (ERD) will be used to model system data and will

- Identify business entities about which data is stored

- Document relevant relationships between the data entities

- Define data attributes

- Be normalized into an effective configuration of entities

The final data model can be found at the end of this chapter in the normalization section. It will be necessary to refer to it throughout the discussion that follows. Some of the techniques described in this chapter cannot be applied until other model components (such as attributes and relationships) have been established. Keep in mind that these techniques are iterative and are not completed in a single step. (Also refer to Appendix B, Model Notation and Symbols.)

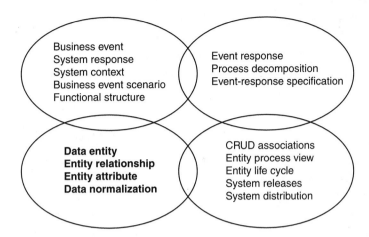

What is the *risk* if a conceptual data model is *not completed*? The database that is eventually implemented may not contain needed elements or may not be configured adequately to support data access requirements for the application currently under development as well as for future applications. A model of the stored data can be tested and validated as behavior and process models are built, while it is relatively easy and much less costly to make adjustments.

6.1 Data Entity

"An entity is a class of real-world things whose role of interaction with the enterprise is well defined" [Yourdon, 1993]. Entities are the building blocks of the data model and the subsequent database. Data entities are defined to hold the persistent data for a system and will provide a basis for tables when the physical database is built. They form the foundation for the identification of relationships and attributes that will complete the data model.

Entities are an abstraction of something found in the problem domain such that each instance or occurrence of the entity will have the same characteristics and will conform to the same set of rules. They define something in the business about which data must be stored to support the business process.

Data entities will hold the data that will be transformed into system outputs in subsequent processing, and they begin to establish the high-level scope of the data to be stored. Some entities represent tangible real-world objects while others have a much more abstract nature. This section will consider the following types of entities (refer to the glossary for definitions and additional discussion).

- Fundamental

- Associative

- Attributive (weak, dependent)

- Supertype

- Subtype

For additional information about the derivation of entities, see Data Normalization later in this chapter.

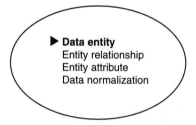

6.1.1 Technique

- Identify fundamental objects in the business area about which data must be stored. Do not restrict your selection to those objects that are necessary for the application currently under study. A broader view is needed to support future applications (schedule and budget may restrict this effort).

- Examine the events that have been identified; events often reveal data entities.

- Establish a key for each entity. The key must be a unique identifier for each occurrence of the entity. Example: A customer key is often the combination of a character and a sequential number and uniquely identifies each customer. It is best not to store data about the entity in the key (smart key).

- Create a textual description of the entity. Example: "A customer is any person or organization that has purchased a product from our company in the last five years." This must clearly identify the business rules of a customer.

- Examine individual entities for common attributes. Move these common attributes (generalization) to a supertype entity (refer to Order and its relationship to Commercial and Individual in the final example).

- Examine individual entities for attributes that are null for some occurrences of the entity. Move these unique attributes (specialization) from the entity to subtype entities (refer to subtypes Commercial and Individual in the final example).

- Add associative entities to the model following the establishment of relationships. Associative entities resolve many-to-many relationships and are also required when a relationship needs to be described by attributes. Refer to Ordered Item in the example. More discussion is included in Data Normalization in this chapter.

- Add attributive entities to hold repeating attributes and groups of repeating attributes (refer to Data Normalization in this chapter for a more thorough discussion).

- Additional entities are created as normalization is performed. Refer to Data Normalization in this chapter for this process.

6.1.2 Example

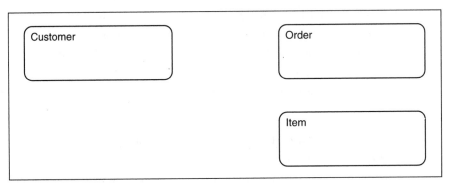

Figure 6.1   Cyber Order System fundamental entities

Other entities that will be identified as the data model evolves as relationships and attributes are added are the following.

- Commercial Order (subtype)

- Individual Order (subtype)

- Item Discount (attributive)

- Item Return (attributive)

- Ordered Item (associative)

6.1.3 Technique Tips

- Define a key as a random collection of characters. Do not define a key to hold data facts (often called a smart key); place the data in an attribute.

- Entities with the same primary key should be examined to determine if they should be combined to form a single entity. Leave them separate if combining them seems to be unnatural in the context of the problem domain.

- Adding associative entities to the model will reveal new attributes and will extend the data model to represent more fully the data needs of the system and the business area and provide a mechanism for verification.

- If an entity has attributes that are null for some of the entity occurrences (that apply to some occurrences of the entity but not to others), consider establishing subtypes to hold those attributes. Also examine existing entities for similarity that would allow the establishment of a supertype to hold common attributes. In the example, some order information does not relate to all orders. Two subtypes were established to document the dependency of those particular attributes on the type of order (commercial or individual).

- In all cases, supertypes and subtypes reveal information about the stored data and provide a greater understanding of the business being modeled. But in an object-oriented environment, these special entity structures are actually implemented as instruments of inheritance.

- A Social Security number uniquely identifies an individual in the United States but typically should not be used as a key, because it allows access to sensitive data and should not be public information as keys typically are.

- Not all entities are discovered in the first pass. Normalization and the addition of relationships to the data model are likely to result in additional entities.

6.2   Entity Relationship

An entity relationship defines the way in which two entities relate to each other in the business and represents a possible association between occurrences of entities. Each occurrence of the relationship corresponds to specific occurrences of the entities. Relationships capture the necessary links between data entities and document the business rules that apply to the relationships.

Each relationship contains both maximum and minimum cardinality at each entity. However, relationship types are named by their maximum cardinality: one-to-one, one-to-many, or many-to-many. Relationships also have a minimum cardinality of either zero or one at each entity; that is, they have either mandatory participation in the relationship or optional participation based on the organization's business rules. It is also possible to have a recursive relationship in which one occurrence of an entity relates to another occurrence of the same entity.

Cardinality will be represented visually when possible using crow's feet for "many," a straight vertical line for "one," and an "O" for optional participation. If cardinality has specific limits, it can be shown by using the minimum and/or maximum values, such as 2:2.

Entity relationships in the ERD provide a navigation path between entities to connect related attributes and begin to document links that must be established in the physical database. They also reveal business events and changes of state of the data entities.

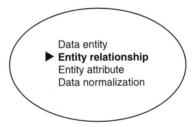

Data entity
▶ **Entity relationship**
Entity attribute
Data normalization

6.2.1 Technique

- Document relationships that are fundamental to the business by considering each pair of entities. These relationships must be useful to the business area under consideration. For example, "Customer places Order" is important because the organization needs to be able to associate a customer with a specific order or an order with a specific customer for purposes of billing or customer service.

- Document maximum cardinality at each end of the relationship. Maximum cardinality is one or many and will begin to document business rules and also names the relationship type.

  Example:

  – One customer can place many orders (one-to-*many*).

  – An order can be placed by only one customer (*one*-to-many).

- Document minimum cardinality at each end of the relationship. Minimum cardinality is zero or one and continues to document business rules.

  Example:

  – An item *may not* have been ordered.

  – An order *must* have at least one item.

- Resolve all many-to-many relationships by establishing an associative entity. The relationships are "many" at the associative entity and "one and only one" at the other ends (see Ordered Item in Figure 6.4).

- Add foreign keys to the entities as needed to implement the relationships. Foreign keys are always established on the "many" side of a relationship pointing toward the "single" side (in the final example, Customer ID is a foreign key placed in Order). In a one-to-one relationship, it is better for them to point toward a required end (mandatory participation), if one exists, rather than toward optional participation.

- Name each relationship. Names are read clockwise, and in most cases only one is needed. A name is necessary because the business rules depend on the nature of the relationship. In the example, "Customer places Order" has very different implications and business rules than would "Customer pays for Order."

6.2.2 Example

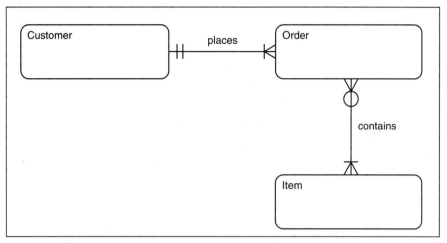

Figure 6.2   Cyber Order System relationships

- One customer can place many orders.

- A particular order can be placed by only one customer.

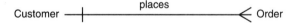

- One customer must have placed at least one order.

- An order must have been placed by at least one customer.

- Other relationship examples:

  "item is assigned an item discount"

  "an order contains order items"

  "an item is contained on an order item"

6.2.3 Technique Tips

- Relationships indicate paths for navigation that are needed to access data. For example, given an order number, the corresponding customer could be accessed using the foreign key Customer ID.

- Relationships often reveal business events, and business events often reveal relationships. Example: Customer places Order.

- Minimum cardinality is zero or one, while maximum cardinality is one or more-than-one (many).

- When determining cardinality (refer to "Customer places Order" in the example), consider a single occurrence of Customer and examine the possible number of orders with which that one customer could be associated. Then reverse the direction and repeat the process for a single Order.

- In the example, a single customer can relate to many orders and, by the definition of a customer given earlier, must have at least one order. A single order can relate to a maximum of one customer (two customers cannot submit the same order), and each order, must have been submitted by only one customer.

- A many-to-many relationship will eventually be resolved in the conceptual model but can be left in the early versions for discussion with the user groups since it most accurately represents the business as they will likely see it.

- Associative entities resulting from a many-to-many relationship add value to the conceptual model because new entities, relationships, and attributes will be revealed and will extend the data model to represent more fully the data needs of the system and the business area.

- There are two variations of keys for associative entities: "single occurrence" and "multiple occurrence." In many cases, a concatenated key made up of the keys from the original many-to-many entities will be unique and therefore sufficient (*Order number* and *Item number* if the same item cannot be repeated in the same order). But in other cases this combination key can repeat and will not work. An additional attribute such as a time stamp or sequential number must be added to the concatenated key. Example: *Order Number* and *Item Number* are not adequate if the same item can occur more than once in the same order (for example, if a second product color is ordered). A sequential line item number could be added to make the key unique: *Order Number, Item Number, Line Item Number.* There are other physical key solutions that are simpler, but conceptually the full key should be shown.

- It is possible that an associative entity will contain only the necessary keys and no other attributes. Conceptually, this is acceptable, because it must be documented whether or not the associative entity is of single or multiple occurrence. Typically, however, something useful will be recorded about the relationship defined in the associative entity—in the example, the quantity of an ordered item.

- Some relationships, such as those for attributive and associative entities, are established during normalization.

- Foreign keys relate to implementation using a relational database and are physical but useful at this level.

6.3 Entity Attribute

Attributes define the properties of a data entity and they record detailed information about the entity that must be stored over time. A data attribute can be a data item that will not be decomposed further (data element) or can be composed of more than one data element (data structure). Address is often a data structure composed of street address, city, state, and zip code.

Attributes will hold the data values of each occurrence of an entity in the subsequent physical database and for the processing that is applied to the data.

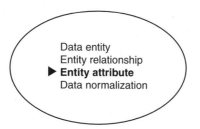

6.3.1 Technique

- In parallel with entity and relationship development, list attributes as they are encountered. Include any piece of information about an entity that will need to be stored over time to support current and future systems. Capture attributes in a list associated with the entity that they describe.

- Apply the rules of normalization as the attributes are placed with an entity.

- Examine the future vision of the business to yield attributes not currently used.

- Define the properties of each attribute. Each attribute is described by the following properties.

  - Domain: those values that are valid (examples: a range of 1–9999; two-character state codes)
  - Data type: alphabetic, numeric, alphanumeric
  - Attribute length: the maximum number of characters allowed
  - Null valid: is it valid for the attribute to be empty?

6.3.2 Example

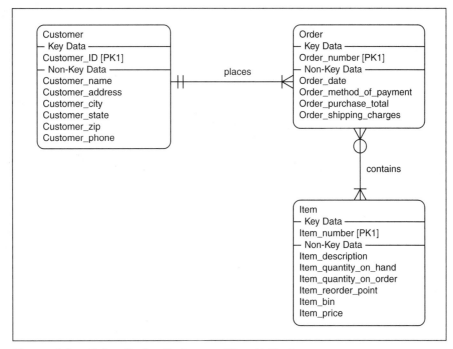

Figure 6.3   Cyber Order System entity attributes

Properties of *Customer name*:

    Data type: character

    Length: 30

    Domain: any alphabetic character and a dash (-)

    Null validity: null not allowed

6.3.3 Technique Tips

- Current forms and reports are good sources of attributes. But keep in mind that a new system is being designed and new ideas are wanted. "Dead wood" should not be carried into the new system.

- If the attribute does not belong to an entity that has already been discovered, add it to a list for now. It may lead to the discovery of a new entity.

- Attributes are best captured in joint design sessions with the user, and those identified by the development team can be verified in joint sessions.

- When an attribute seems to have its own attributes (that is, various data elements that describe it), it may need to be elevated to the status of an entity.

6.4 Data Normalization

Normalization of data produces the proper configuration of entities along with the proper placement of attributes. This reduces redundancy, eliminates data anomalies, and provides a data architecture that supports the effective and efficient retrieval and modification of data (CRUD).

Normalization is a formal approach to organizing and assigning attributes to create stable, flexible, and adaptive entities [Whitten and Bentley, 1998]. In this guide, it applies rules by which data is taken to first normal form, second normal form, and third normal form.

Normalization is applied during the creation of the business area or system data model to support the development of an effective, efficient data model. This will also have future value since normalized data can be integrated much more easily than unnormalized data.

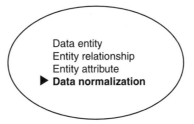

Data entity
Entity relationship
Entity attribute
▶ **Data normalization**

6.4.1 Technique

- *First normal form:* Remove a repeating attribute (or attributes) to its own entity (typically called an attributive or weak or dependent entity and shown as a double-lined entity in the example); the key will be the key from the original entity plus a key for establishing uniqueness within the repeating group. The relationship is one to many or many to many. If the relationship is many to many, an associative entity will be needed rather than an attributive entity. Example: Item Discount is an attributive entity of Item created to hold the multiple (repeating) occurrences of promotional discount information (see example).

- *Second normal form:* For any entity with a primary key consisting of more than one attribute (concatenated key), remove attributes that are dependent on only part of the key. The part of the concatenated key on which the attributes are dependent becomes the key of the new entity. The original key does not change. The relationship is many to one. In the example, if Item Description were included in Item Discount, it would be dependent only on the Item Number and not the Date Begin and must be removed to the Item entity.

- *Third normal form:* Remove attributes that are dependent on another non-key attribute. The new entity has the non-key attribute from the original entity as its key. The non-key attribute stays in the original entity as a foreign key. The relationship is many to one. This is similar to establishing second normal form except that the dependency is on a non-key attribute rather than on part of the primary key. In the example, if Item Bin Location were included in Item, it would be dependent on Item Bin (a non-key attribute) and not on the primary key and must be removed to an entity that holds information about the warehouse (not included in this data model).

- *Many-to-many relationships:* Resolve all many-to-many relationships by establishing an associative entity (shown with an embedded triangle). This needs to be done during requirements definition, because new entities, relationships, and attributes will be revealed. The relationships are "many" at the associative entity and one and only one at the other ends (see Ordered Item in the example).

6.4.2 Example

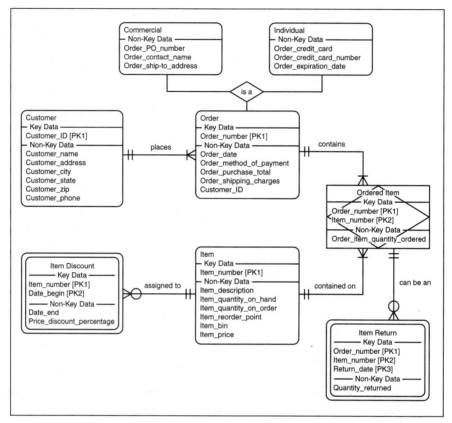

Figure 6.4   Cyber Order System normalized data model

6.4.3 Technique Tips

- A repeating attribute (or group of attributes) occurs when, for a single value of the key, more than one value can occur in the repeating attribute (violation of first normal form). In the examples below, discount information can occur many times for a single item (note {repeating group}) and return data can occur more than once for Ordered Item. The repeating data should be moved to an entity of its own, as shown in Figure 6.4.

Item	*Ordered Item*
Item_number (PK)	Order_number (PK)
Item_description	Item_number (PK)
Item_quantity_on_hand	Order_item_quantity_ordered
Item_quantity_on_order	{Return_date
Item_reorder_point	Quantity_returned}
Item_bin	
Item_price	
{Date_begin	
Date_end	
Price_discount_percentage}	

- An attribute that is dependent on only part of a concatenated key is in violation of second normal form. In the example below, *Item_description* depends on only the *Item_number* and not the full, concatenated key. Item_description should be moved to the Item entity.

  Item_number (PK)
  Date_begin (PK)
  Item_description
  Date_end
  Price_discount_percentage

- An attribute that is dependent on a non-key attribute is in violation of third normal form. In the example below, *Item_bin_location* is dependent on *Item_bin* and not on any part of the entity key. Warehouse information such as Item_bin_location should be stored in a separate entity.

  Item_number (PK)
  Item_description
  Item_quantity_on_hand
  Item_quantity_on_order
  Item_reorder_point
  Item_bin
  Item_bin_location
  Item_price

- Normalization of the data does not have to follow in order from first to third normal form. Third normal form could be considered first. However, since placing data in first normal form may create an entity with concatenated keys, examination for a second normal form problem naturally follows.

- It is recommended that a final pass be made through the entities following the order of first, second, and then third normal form.

- Repeating groups are often resolved with an associative entity rather than an attributive entity. In the data model example, Items would be a repeating attribute in Order and would be moved to an attributive entity called Ordered Item along with quantity ordered. But when the Item entity is added, Ordered Item becomes an associative entity.

Project Management Tips—System Data

- Development of the data model should be conducted in parallel with the analysis and specification of business events.
- As with the discovery of events, use this effort to examine the proposed system from a real-world perspective and to involve the user group.
- Don't expect to find all of the entities during this phase of data model development. Normalization will likely produce new entities.
- Keep in mind that these activities are part of an iterative strategy and that this work will be revisited as more is learned about the proposed system.
- Normalization is not just a separate step but is applied as the model develops. The team should verify the correctness of the model frequently.
- Keep this effort conceptual and real-world. Encourage the team to avoid thinking of a physical implementation.
- More than one configuration of the model can emerge. Team meetings may be needed to resolve conflicts about model structure.

CHAPTER SEVEN

System Process

- **7.1 Event Response**
- **7.2 Process Decomposition**
- **7.3 Event-Response Specification**

The models developed thus far do not provide sufficient detail from which to develop or generate system programs. Event responses have been represented as "black boxes" and system inputs and outputs have been named but not defined to the attribute level. The process modeling further specifies the system components with Data Flow Diagrams (DFDs).

> **Event response:** The complete, planned response the system will make when invoked to respond to an event. It is idle before being invoked, returns to an idle state when processing is completed, and leaves the business in a consistent state.

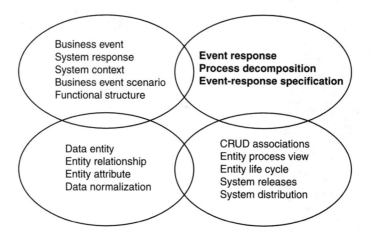

7.1   Event Response

These diagrams document the inputs and outputs of each event response. By definition of an event response, these interfaces are with external agents and data stores only. No data is passed directly between event responses, thus creating an architecture with relatively low coupling.

An Event Diagram is a DFD that has a single process. There is one Event Diagram for each event response in the System Response Table (SRT). The process is named exactly as the event response in the table. All interfaces to external agents and to data entities are shown, and the data entities are named exactly as in the data model.

This is the first time in the system development life cycle that a detailed examination of the interface with the data model for each event response is completed. It is also the first significant use of DFDs (refer to Appendix B, Model Notation and Symbols). These diagrams may be decomposed later in the life cycle to reveal more and more detail and to partition for possible distribution of both data and processes. They are also paired with Entity Process Views (EPVs) during interaction modeling.

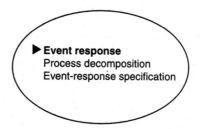

▶ Event response
Process decomposition
Event-response specification

7.1.1 Technique

- For each row in the SRT, create a DFD process with the event-response name from the table (Figure 7.1 is for the first row in the table).

- Add external agents to the diagram. These will be agents outside of the system that either provide data to the process or receive information from the process (refer to the SRT).

- Add the data flows between the process and the external agents. Data flows into the process represent data provided by the user or by a device such as a sensor. Data flows out to an external agent represent information produced by the event response. Some methodologies show rejection flows (the result of failed validation) here while others do not.

- Add the data stores representing the data entities from the data model that are needed to provide stored data to the process and/or that will be updated by the process.

- Add the data flows to and from the data stores showing the flow of data attributes as needed by the process or as produced by the event-response process to update a data store.

7.1.2 Example

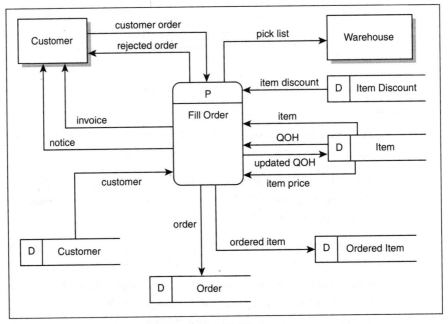

Figure 7.1   Cyber Order System Event Diagram

7.1.3 Risk if Not Completed

For each response to an event, data required from outside the system, the use of stored data by the process, and the information that is produced by the process must all be documented, one way or another.

7.1.4 Technique Tips

- This is a conceptual model and not a physical one. Things such as "Faxed order" and "Phoned order" should be replaced by the more abstract form "Order."

- An external agent represents a role, organization, department, or other conceptual source or destination of data.

- A data flow represents the flow of data attributes from one DFD component to another and is unidirectional.

- A process represents the transformation of data following a set of business rules.

- A data store represents a data entity from the data model and stores data over time.

- A DFD shows all possible paths of data as it is being transformed from input to output. It is much like a road map in that not all paths are necessarily traversed for a specific occurrence of a trigger.

- Data flows must begin or end at a process.

- A data flow is named with an adjective/noun that describes the composition of the data.

- A process is named with an active verb/object that describes the data transformation that takes place.

- A name of a data flow must change as it passes through a process to represent the transformation that takes place. If no transformation takes place, the data flow should have bypassed the process.

- The rule of data conservation: Each process in the DFD must have sufficient input for the creation of its output.

- The analyst must understand the transformation rules of a process before decisions can be made regarding the data requirements of the process.

- When using the methods in this handbook, there is a one-to-one mapping of event responses in the SRT to Event Diagrams.

- An Event Diagram contains all of the processing required to produce the necessary output of an event response when a trigger is received. It is in an idle state when the trigger is received, and when all processing is complete it returns to an idle state awaiting another instance of the trigger.

- Each event response is an elementary process that must leave the business in a consistent state when processing is completed. For example, in a product distribution system, when the third stop is completed, the first and second stops must be checked for proper status.

- It doesn't take long to draw and specify an event diagram, but it may take awhile to gain sufficient understanding to complete one.

- Control flow is typically not shown on a DFD. When it is shown, it requires a special notation not shown in this book. One notation uses a broken line, and another uses a heavy, bold line. A textual description of the nature of the control data is recommended.

7.2 Process Decomposition

The leveling (decomposition) of a DFD provides a more detailed view of the processing and data requirements contained in the parent process. It also provides partitioning that can be used to distribute processing and data for system architectures such as Client/Server.

A leveled DFD contains multiple processes that describe the total processing of the parent. These processes exchange data with each other, with data stores, and with external agents as necessary to produce the required outputs. Typically, only complex or poorly understood event responses require this decomposition. Many analysis teams completely ignore this level of the diagram.

These DFDs, when described by data flow and process specifications, document the detail of the complex processing necessary to develop a working system. They lie at the bottom of the process model hierarchy.

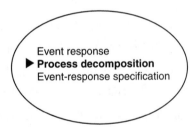

7.2.1 Technique

- Identify the processes that are required to generate the output specified in the Event Diagram. A list will work well at this time.

- Identify the processing required to get data from external agents including validation. Add to the process list.

- Begin to create the leveled DFD by placing the processes generally from upper left to lower right in the sequence of execution. Conceptual (rather than physical) processes can often execute in parallel rather than in series and should be shown in parallel whenever possible.

- Place the external agents near the processes that interface with them; add the input and output data flows as in the parent process. Since the decomposition represents the entire processing of the parent, the inputs and outputs should balance.

- Write the structured English describing the transformation logic of each process in the leveled DFD. This will help identify the data required by each process.

- Add the required data stores and the related data flows to the diagram needed to support the processing. These data flows must balance with the parent.

- Add data flows between the processes as required. Execute processes in parallel when possible. For example, Generate Pick List, Update Inventory, and Calculate Charges can execute at the same time with the same "Valid Order" data while Generate Invoice and Generate Order are dependent on Calculate Charges for the data flow "Charges" and must be shown serially.

7.2.2 Example

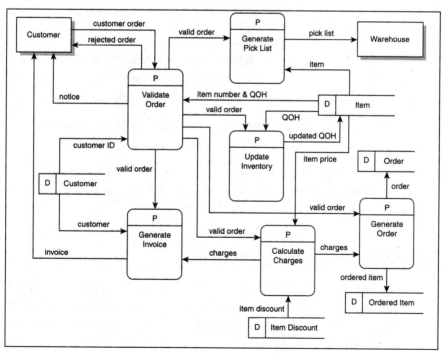

Figure 7.2   Cyber Order System Leveled Event Diagram

7.2.3 Risk if Not Completed

The processing detail of complex event responses is not examined and documented and therefore may not be sufficiently understood. This can affect subsequent development efforts, estimating and scheduling, and the partitioning of processes and data required in a distributed architecture such as Client/Server.

7.2.4 Technique Tips

- Typically, only complex or poorly understood event responses require this decomposition. Most of the custodial functions for the database will not be modeled below the Event Diagram.

- Each flow to or from the parent process represents some processing and can be used to begin the decomposition.

- Data that can be obtained from a data store is not passed from one process to another. In a *conceptual* model such as this, the representation of data available to each process because of prior processing is a *physical* matter dependent on the language and is not defined until later phases.

- Data passed between processes should be confined to data entity keys necessary to define occurrences of an entity and/or data generated by the sending process that is not available from stored data. Physically it may be done differently, but conceptually, since access to stored data costs nothing (is error-free and takes no time), stored data should be the source when possible.

- A process should be shown to execute in parallel when possible, dependent on only those processes that produce data it requires.

- When difficulty is experienced putting together a leveled DFD, the business being modeled and the data required for processing are probably not well understood.

7.3   Event-Response Specification

Specification of the DFDs provides detailed information about the model that is necessary for subsequent construction of the system programs. It forces the development team and user group to new levels of understanding and validation of the data and processing.

Both the processing logic and the content of the data flows are specified to augment the diagram. Techniques such as Action Diagrams and structured English are used to document the process logic (called minispecs or process specs) while a simple list of attributes and data structures describes the data flow content.

This is the most atomic level of the DFD. The granularity of the data and the processing logic can be sufficient for them to be used to develop code in later phases.

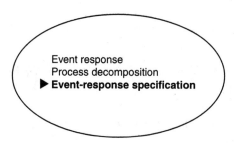

7.3.1 Technique

- Using structured English as shown in the example, describe the logic for each of the lowest-level processes. If only an Event Diagram was developed, specify that process. If an Event Diagram was leveled, specify the processes at the lowest level. Use "BR" to document business-rule logic.

- Describe the content of each data flow on each Event Diagram even if the process was leveled. As shown in the example, this includes attributes from the data model and data structures (groups of attributes) that have been defined in the data dictionary. Include only data that is required by the process (see rules in Technique Tips).

- Examine the Entity Life Cycle Diagram (ELCD) to determine the pre-state and post-state values of the entities involved. The event-response logic is responsible for validating, preserving, and setting the appropriate states.

- The structured English and data flow definitions can be documented in a CASE repository or in a project library maintained in a word processor if a CASE tool is not used.

7.3.2 Example

This example is for the *Fill Order* Event Diagram, not the leveled diagram. When a leveled diagram is specified, pseudocode is written for each of the decomposed processes.

Validate order

    customer on file

    valid date not later than current date

    not null: PO, contact name, credit card information

    {item on file

    numeric quantity }

If invalid, reject for re-entry

Generate next order number

For each valid item

    Using valid order

        If quantity on hand less than quantity ordered generate notice

        End If

    Using valid order

        get item information (Item)

        add to pick list

    Using valid order

        get QOH (Item)

        update QOH

    Using valid order

        get item price (Item)

        get price discount percentage for order date (Item Discount)

        calculate charges (BR 1)

    Using valid order and charges

        generate ordered item (Ordered Item)

End For

Using order number

    generate pick list

Using valid order and charges

    generate order (Order)

Using valid order and charges

    get customer information (Customer)

    generate invoice

BR 1: ((((Item price * Item price discount) * quantity ordered) * tax rate)

Customer order =	Ship-to address =	Pick list =
customer ID	recipient name	order number
date order sent	street address	{item number
ship-to address	city	item description
PO number	state	item bin
contact name	zip	quantity ordered}
credit card		
{item number	Credit card =	
description of item	credit card name	
quantity ordered	credit card number	
catalog price}	credit card expiration date	
Notice =	Invoice =	
order number	customer ID	
customer ID	customer name	
customer phone	ship-to address	
date order sent	{item number	
item number	item description	
item description	order item quantity ordered	
order item quantity ordered	item price}	

7.3.3 Risk if Not Completed

Someone somewhere will have to understand what data attributes and process logic are required if this system is to be developed. Failure to develop such understanding in this phase simply pushes the work to later phases, when the user groups may not be as accessible and the developer may be more involved with the physical components of the system.

7.3.4 Technique Tips

- Use the following notation when describing a data flow.

    { } to indicate repeating attributes or groups of attributes

    [ ] to indicate that only one attribute from the list is selected

    ( ) to indicate that the attribute(s) is (are) optional

< > to indicate that one or more attributes from the list are selected

BR   to indicate business-rule logic

- Process specification can be defined at various levels of detail from high-level bullets to code-level logic constructs such as If-Then-Else.

- When a *data flow* is named as an attribute from the data model, it does not need further definition.

- When a *data flow* represents an entire record being read (all attributes required) from a data store or written to a data store, name it the same as the data store and it needs no further definition.

Project Management Tips—System Process

- There is little advantage in having more than one person work on a single event response. It is typical for one team member to work on more than one.
- There is a tendency to shortcut this part of the requirements. The detail can become tedious. However, the team must understand and document the system to a level dictated by these models while the user is fully involved. Otherwise, it will be left for the programmer to figure it out without sufficient user participation.
- Each event response can be considered to be a subsystem with its own user interface, business rules, and output products. This provides flexibility in the assignment of tasks, the monitoring of work, and the reassignment of resources as the project progresses.
- The leveling (decomposition) of an Event Diagram is typically not needed. Most event responses are simple enough to require specification only in the pseudocode.
- The leveling of an event DFD is time-consuming and requires a detailed understanding of the process and of the data flow. It will likely be beneficial for complex processes but not worth the resources for most event responses.
- The structure of the pseudocode (structured English) can vary on the basis of the preferences and needs of each team. An alternative to the "For Loop" in the example follows.

> For each valid item
> > Generate notice when quantity on hand is insufficient to fill order
> > Add item to pick list
> > Update quantity on hand
> > Calculate charges (BR 1)
> > Create *Ordered Item*
> > End For

- The data flow definitions become data structures at the programming level.
- Separating the business rules (BR) from the pseudocode makes it easier to modify the specification when the business rules change.
- A CASE tool, or at the very least a good drawing tool, is necessary when models are being built and maintained.

CHAPTER EIGHT

Data/Process Interaction

- ■ **8.1 CRUD Associations**
- ■ **8.2 Entity Process View**
- ■ **8.3 Entity Life Cycle**

Data stored in a database is of little value to a user unless it is processed. When processes are executed, they are executed against data. This interaction between the data and the processing is what produces an output product that is of value to the user. Three techniques for checking and validating the data and process interaction will be examined.

Business event
System response
System context
Business event scenario
Functional structure

Event response
Process decomposition
Event-response specification

Data entity
Entity relationship
Entity attribute
Data normalization

CRUD associations
Entity process view
Entity life cycle
System releases
System distribution

8.1 CRUD Associations

The acronym CRUD represents the custodial functions of a typical database entity—that is, Create, Read, Update, and Delete. Each table or file in a database must have these functions from the system under design and development or from another system. The CRUD matrix (also Data/Process Matrix or Entity/Event-Response Matrix) provides a means of examining the interaction between data entities in the data model and event responses from the System Response Table (SRT) by documenting which of the four functions each event response provides for each data entity. Any data entity without all four CRUD functions will require further examination of the proposed system for missing functionality.

The CRUD matrix provides a means of examining the interaction between data entities and event responses and validating the completeness of the proposed system design. It also documents data dependencies between event responses for use when designing multiple releases of a system.

The CRUD matrix reveals the way in which the data and the processing interact. It also is used during early design to partition the system for multiple releases.

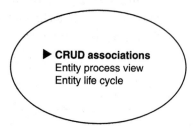

▶ **CRUD associations**
Entity process view
Entity life cycle

8.1.1 Technique

- Build a matrix with the data entities on one axis and the event responses on the other.

- At each intersection of a row and column (each cell), record which of the four CRUD functions the event response provides for that data entity (from zero to all four).

- Examine each row or column, whichever has the data entities, for all four CRUD functions. If any functions are missing for an entity, it must be determined whether it is the responsibility of the system under development or another system.

- Note from the example that instances of Item are not created in the system as defined here. Item was not shown to be outside of the system in the context diagram (where another system would create these instances), so there is no apparent explanation for the fact that Item instances are not created.

8.1.2 Example

Table 8.1.   Cyber Order System CRUD Matrix

Event Response	Customer	Item Discount	Item	Order	Ordered Item
Fill order	R	R	RU	C	C
Process return	R		RU	R	R
Add customer	C				
Record discount information		CU	R		
Produce item availability	R		R		
Generate daily sales report	R			R	R

C = Create, R = Read, U = Update

8.1.3 Risk if Not Completed

Required processes that are not evident from the business event analysis might be missed. Also, a means of examining data dependencies between event responses would not be available.

8.1.4 Technique Tips

- Some methodologies suggest listing only the most significant function in each cell. It is suggested here that any and all of the functions that are provided by the event response be shown.

- Use the event diagrams when building the CRUD matrix since they show all interfaces with the data entities.

- Refer to the process specs when building the CRUD matrix because they offer detailed information about interfaces with the data entities.

- The CRUD matrix shows data dependencies. For example, when an event response is reading a data entity, it can be determined which other event response (or responses) creates or updates that entity. The functionality requiring the read cannot be implemented without the create and update functions.

8.2 Entity Process View

An Entity Process View (EPV) is a combination of an event response and the corresponding fragment of the data model that is required for processing. It consists of the entities shown in the event diagrams along with any other entities required by a relationship.

The EPV isolates the part of the data model required by a particular event response, thus reducing the data view to only those entities and relationships actually required by the event processing. It is easier to think about data and the required processing of a single event response when only subsets of the entire data model and process model are targeted.

It is a technique for examining the interaction between the system processing and the static data to verify consistency and completeness. The EPV described here is similar to the Entity Model View described in the Ernst & Young Navigator methodology.

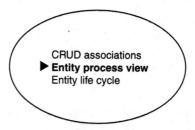

CRUD associations
▶ **Entity process view**
Entity life cycle

8.2.1 Technique

- Examine the data stores of an event diagram and identify the corresponding entities in the data model.

- Copy those entities from the data model along with the relationships between them (see the example).

- Also copy any other entity that is at the end of a required relationship with one of the original entities. For example, the Customer entity in the example.

- Verify that the event-response process specifications consider the many occurrences at the end of one-to-many relationships as well as required and optional minimum cardinalities.

8.2.2 Example

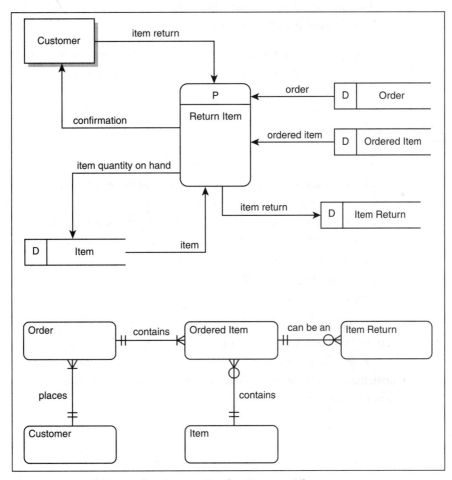

Figure 8.1   Cyber Order System Entity Process View

8.2.3 Risk if Not Completed

An opportunity to discover obscure processing requirements might be missed. Also, a more general opportunity to focus on a relatively small part of the entire system for the purpose of validating completeness of the system response to a business event would be lost.

8.2.4 Technique Tips

- If time permits, it is valuable to combine, on a single page, both the event diagram and the data model fragment for examination.

- A "many" maximum cardinality requires iteration (looping) in the process logic for each occurrence of the single entity.

- A "required" minimum cardinality might indicate that the event response should create an instance of an entity or require the presence of an instance of an entity.

8.3 Entity Life Cycle

A state diagram relates events and states. When an event is received, the next state depends on the current state as well as the event; a change of state caused by an event is called a transition. A state diagram is a graph whose nodes are states and whose directed arcs are transitions labeled by event names. . . . The state diagram specifies the state sequence caused by an event sequence. If an object is in a state and an event labeling one of its transitions occurs, the object enters the state on the target end of the transition. [Rumbaugh et al., 1991]

An entity's life cycle is the set of state transitions that an entity undergoes from its inception through its ultimate obsolescence. The study of an entity life cycle is the documentation of the possible relevant states and the events that move the entity from one state to another. This documentation is typically in the form of a diagram.

Early examination of an entity life cycle can help discover events in the business area or can provide an understanding of the interaction between the entities and the events when used late in the analysis phase.

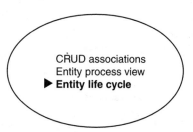

CRUD associations
Entity process view
▶ **Entity life cycle**

8.3.1 Technique

- With help from the user, list the states of the system's major data entities (see the example).

- For those data entities with a rich set of states, build an Entity Life Cycle Diagram (ELCD). An ELCD represents the sequence of valid entity states, depicts the dependencies between states, and documents the business event that causes a change in state.

- Compare for completeness the events from the ELCD (see example in this section) with the event list developed early in the analysis phase (Chapter 5).

8.3.2 Example

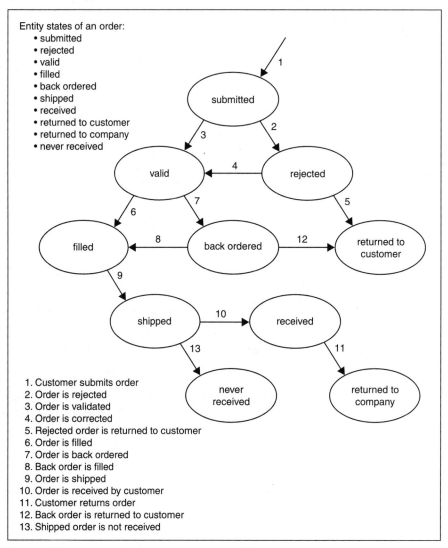

Entity states of an order:
- submitted
- rejected
- valid
- filled
- back ordered
- shipped
- received
- returned to customer
- returned to company
- never received

1. Customer submits order
2. Order is rejected
3. Order is validated
4. Order is corrected
5. Rejected order is returned to customer
6. Order is filled
7. Order is back ordered
8. Back order is filled
9. Order is shipped
10. Order is received by customer
11. Customer returns order
12. Back order is returned to customer
13. Shipped order is not received

Figure 8.2   Cyber Order System Entity Life Cycle Diagram

8.3.3 Risk if Not Completed

An opportunity may be missed to gain further understanding of the processing requirements of the proposed system as they relate to the data and to discover overlooked events.

8.3.4 Technique Tips

- An entity state represents a time window in the life cycle of an entity.

- States within a single ELCD must be mutually exclusive.

- Often, more than one life cycle will exist for a single entity.

- For our order processing system case study, the ELCD reveals many events that have not been documented so far. It should be obvious to the development team that it has some work to do.

Project Management Tips—Data/Process Interaction

- The CRUD matrix is referred to as "process-data matrix" or something similar in much of the current literature.
- Use the CRUD matrix to look for missing functions. Each data entity must have create, read, update, and delete functions in the proposed system or another system.
- Use the CRUD matrix to verify that each event response is doing everything it should. This matrix offers a second perspective on system functionality and data usage and can be compared with the pseudocode of each event diagram.
- The EPV provides a mechanism for crosschecking of business rules expressed in the data model and their implementation in the event responses. In the example, a customer is required for each order (the customer end of the order/customer relationship shows that participation is required). Make sure the requirement is specified in the pseudocode.
- Building the ELCD is typically most valuable for key entities that have a rich set of states, such as Order in the cyber order system in this book. For the initial examination of each entity, just list the states.
- Business events cause states to change. The ELCD can lead to discovery of new events and verification of existing ones.
- An event response must leave the business in a consistent state. This diagram provides a way of examining this requirement by indicating the "before and after" states of an event.
- This diagram forces a level of understanding of the relationship between business states and business events

CHAPTER NINE

Transition to Physical Design

- **9.1 System Releases**
- **9.2 System Distribution**
- **9.3 Conceptual Event Models to Physical Models**

One of the most popular criticisms of the structured development methodologies has been that transition from the conceptual model of the analysis phase to the physical model of the design phase is not a natural one. It is supposedly difficult to convert a network diagram such as the DFD to hierarchical structure charts.

When a system is partitioned by business events, however, a middle-out rather than a top-down approach is followed and the resulting subsystems are simpler. By using the event diagram for all event responses, most of which are not decomposed, the development of structure charts from DFDs is minimized to a relatively small percentage of the total system.

When the system analysis identifies and defines a large number of events to which the system must respond, the proposed system should be partitioned into multiple applications or releases. This will allow development to be scheduled into projects of a few months' length. The transition to design documents this project content based on system priorities and data dependence.

119

The event responses have low coupling characteristics and are very independent. They can be developed and tested individually, simplifying project management. This partitioning scheme provides excellent traceability back to the original business events defined by the users since the event constructs defined in analysis are persistent through design and construction.

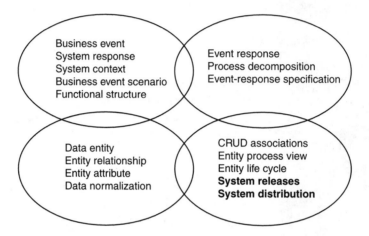

9.1   System Releases

Some of the event responses will typically have higher priorities than will others. These *system priorities* should be documented and then used to define an order of development of the system partitions. But this is not the only factor that must be considered. While event-partitioned systems have fairly low coupling, they still can have strong *data dependencies* and these dependencies must take precedence over business needs to preserve data integrity. The creation and updating of entity instances must be included if the entity is read by other event responses. System release information can be documented in the System Response Table (SRT).

The CRUD matrix can contribute significantly to the task of determining data dependencies between the various event-response partitions of the system. Each process that creates or updates a data entity must be in place in the system when functions using that data are implemented. The application model begins the transition to the design phase.

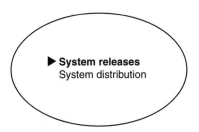

▶ **System releases**
System distribution

9.1.1 Technique

- Determine which output products must be delivered in the first phase of the system and the event responses that produce them.

- Entity by entity, examine those event responses that produce high-priority outputs, and using the CRUD matrix, identify additional event responses that create or update the entities required for the production of the required outputs.

- Considering priorities and data dependencies, partition the event responses into releases with development lengths of no more than six months, if possible, and document in a table similar to the SRT in Chapter 5 (see Table 9.1).

- Using the analysis models, identify those event responses that have user interface components. These event responses are candidates for prototyping.

9.1.2 Example

Table 9.1. Cyber Order System—System Release Table

Business Event	Source	Trigger	Event Response	System Release
Customer places order	Customer	Order	Fill Order	1
Customer returns item	Customer	Item	Process return	1
Person requests customer status	Candidate customer	Customer status request	Add customer	1

(continued)

Table 9.1. *(continued)*

Business Event	Source	Trigger	Event Response	System Release
Management submits item discount information	Management	Discount information	Record discount information	1
Customer inquires about item availability	Customer	Item availability request	Produce item availability	1
Time to generate daily sales report		(temporal)	Generate daily sales report	1

9.1.3 Risk if Not Completed

When projects are defined for time periods longer than a few months, the risk of failure increases significantly. It is important, when possible, to divide the total system effort into smaller, more manageable applications.

The CRUD matrix contains important information about the use and production of data by each event-response partition of the proposed system. This information is vital for the definition of applications within a system having a large number of event responses, and no model offers more than the CRUD matrix.

9.1.4 Technique Tips

- For a system with a large number of partitions and data entities, this is no easy task. A team session using matrix management software and projection equipment can develop, in real time, a matrix representing the various system releases.

- If "Produce Item Availability" and "Generate Daily Sales Report" are required in release 1, then event responses "Fill Order," "Process Return," and "Add Customer" are also needed to create and update the tables being read by the two reporting functions.

- "Record Discount Information" is also required in release 1 because it creates instances of Item Discount that are read by "Fill Order."

9.2 System Distribution

A distributed system consists of multiple processors working together to support the information needs of an organization. This implies that the data and processes will be distributed over several processors, introducing a number of design and control complications. In the ideal distributed system, the data and processing power are located in the most efficient location. A very sophisticated system infrastructure is needed to make such an ideal system possible. This infrastructure may introduce multiple servers on different machines running different operating systems, multiple Database Management Systems, and multiple vendors.

When parts of a system are distributed, especially into three-tier architectures, the complexity of the system increases significantly. Over time, the distributed configuration of a partitioned system will likely need to be changed as an organization's business needs and technology options change.

> Other considerations are more subtle. For example, an application developer constructing an application to run on a single machine may assume that communications between components are enacted as simple call statements, and that any message (call) sent by one component will be received successfully by the component to which it is sent. In a distributed application, the communications may be implemented as messages that travel long distances over wires or cable with a resultant higher likelihood of failure. The developer may choose to include additional error handling logic to provide for such possibilities. [Bohl, 1995]

As an information system becomes more and more fragmented in the three-tier architectures, having a stable, logical (conceptual) model of the system that is not affected by the changing physical configuration becomes increasingly important.

Conceptual models can be used as the basis for physical system configuration derivation and, regardless of the dynamic nature of the physical system, offer a stable representation of the system requirements.

The methods in this section document the location of conceptual system use along with the parts of the system (data and process) that are needed at each location. Physical implementation considerations are not addressed by these models.

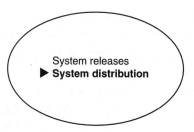

9.2.1 Technique

- List the locations that will require part or all of the system's event responses.

- Expand the list by decomposing each location by functional area and record the number of users in each area.

- Develop a table with the event responses as rows and the location functional areas as columns.

- Mark each cell that identifies a location that requires a specific event response (users will provide this information).

- Develop a table with the data entities as rows and the location functional areas as columns.

- Using the CRUD matrix as a reference from event response to data entity, mark each cell that identifies a location that requires a specific data entity; use the CRUD notation in this table.

- For example, it is determined that Chicago distribution needs "Produce item availability" (they certainly need much more, but that will come in later releases). From the CRUD matrix, it can be seen that the data entities "Customer" and "Item" are also needed as read-only.

9.2.2 Example

Location list:
Chicago
distribution (4)
Indianapolis
order entry (5)
customer service (3)
inventory control (3)
purchasing (3)
Dallas
customer service (4)

Table 9.2.   Cyber Order System Event-Response Distribution Matrix

Event Response	Chicago Distribution	Indy Order Entry	Indy Customer Service	Indy Inventory Control	Indy Purchasing	Dallas Customer Service
Fill order		√				
Process return			√			√
Add customer		√	√			√
Record discount information		√				
Produce item availability	√	√	√	√	√	√
Generate daily sales report			√	√	√	√

Table 9.3.   Cyber Order System Data Entity Distribution Matrix

Data Entity	Chicago Distribution	Indy Order Entry	Indy Customer Service	Indy Inventory Control	Indy Purchasing	Dallas Customer Service
Customer	R	CR	CR	R	R	CR
Item discount		CU				
Item	R	RU	RU	R	R	RU
Order		C	R	R	R	R
Ordered item		C	R	R	R	R

C = Create, R = Read, U = Update

Variations of Tables 9.1 through 9.3 and the accompanying lists can be found in *Systems Analysis and Design Methods* [Whitten and Bentley, 1998], pages 266–279.

9.2.3 Risk if Not Completed

Someone somewhere will have to investigate and document the distributed usage of the system. The later in the delivery process this is done, the higher the risk. It is most effectively accomplished while the users are involved in the early joint sessions.

9.2.4 Technique Tips

- Whitten and Bentley [1998] advocate location network diagrams at this time.

- If more information about the location aspect of the distributed system is needed, this is the phase in which to capture it since joint sessions are in progress and the user is closely involved.

- The data entity distribution matrix could be marked with a checkmark, but the CRUD functions add value to the table.

- It is not significant for system distribution when a row does not have all of the CRUD functionality. It just means that some of the operations on an entity will not be distributed.

9.3 Conceptual Event Models to Physical Models

Conceptual models generated during requirements definition are, by definition, nonphysical. They represent abstractions of the physical business world they represent. An "order" is defined rather than a "telephone order," "mail order," or "internet order." Little attention is given to physical architecture such as three-tier client/server or mainframe platforms. Output content is defined without regard to screen or report format.

As the design phase is addressed, the physical design of the system is resolved. Many decisions must be made regarding security, screen design, platform, distribution, network choices, database design, and other elements of the system.

What the system must accomplish has been established (for some of the event responses, others may be in progress), and the development team must move the system toward a physical solution. For example, the physical network choices can be based partly on the distribution models while the conceptual data model is input to development of the physical database model.

Many of the design decisions can be made on an event-by-event basis. The system processing has been partitioned into responses to events and, these responses can be designed, built, and tested one by one. Also, using the event diagrams, each data flow to or from an external agent represents, for example, all or part of a physical screen, report, sensor data stream, or control output. For on-line applications, a menu structure based on the events being implemented must be designed.

While there may be a significant effort directed toward system infrastructure during design, the majority of the resources will be expended on the production of the application that has been modeled during the definition of requirements and is based on events. Since the requirements gathering effort is iterative and can produce a stream of event responses (rather than all being available for design at one time), the transition to design can occur one event at a time and the system can be implemented incrementally as system releases.

When physical development will use an object orientation, it is recommended that the requirements follow an object-partitioning scheme.

Project Management Tips—Transition to Physical Design

- It is recommended by many software specialists that projects have a maximum duration of six to eight months. This limits the business change that occurs during the life of the project.
- The user will likely dictate which functionality is necessary as a minimum release. The CRUD matrix helps determine which other event responses must be included on the basis of data dependencies.
- Use the CRUD matrix to examine the data dependencies between event responses.
- Use the SRT to document the releases of the proposed system.
- For a system with a large number of partitions and data entities, this is no easy task. A team session using matrix management software and projection equipment can develop, in real time, a matrix representing the various system releases.
- If more information about the location aspect of the distributed system is needed, this is the phase in which to capture it since joint sessions are in progress and the user is closely involved.
- At this point in the project, the distribution of conceptual functions and conceptual data is being examined. The physical aspects of this distribution are not known at this time. The information captured in these requirements will be used when physical decisions are made in the physical design phase.

PART III

Estimating Software Projects

Historically, the size of software projects, measured by time and cost, has been poorly estimated. Ironically, even though management has complained bitterly about missed schedules and budgets, they have offered little time and few resources for the analysis of historical project data so that the estimating process could be improved.

In the United States, fewer than 9 percent of companies use metrics to measure and monitor software development, according to a 1997 poll of 1,100 companies by market research firm Rubin Systems Inc. On a list of nineteen issues that included recruitment, productivity, and project management, metrics rated dead last. What's more, three out of four measurement programs fail, according to research by the Yankee Group, translating into 1.5 percent to 3.7 percent of IT expenditures being wasted. Many IT management teams lack either the experience or the will to ensure the success of a performance tracking system." [*Information Week Online*, 1999]

Function Point Estimates and Events

An event-driven approach to the definition of requirements dovetails with function point counting practices to form a natural estimating technique. The event models reveal most of the components needed to make a function point estimate.

The discussion in this chapter (based on Release 4.0) does not cover the topic of function point estimating to a level that would be obtained by certification in the counting practices. Also, a more comprehensive description of the practices is offered by the International Function Point Users Group [IFPUG, 1994]. However, the discussion here is intended to be sufficient to conduct a parallel pilot case study to assess its merits.

Some material in this chapter has been reprinted from *Estimating Software Costs* (Capers Jones, © 1998) with permission of The McGraw-Hill Companies.

10.1 Difficulty of Estimating Software Projects

So why is estimating the schedule and budget of software projects so difficult? Estimation of software projects has always been a difficult and largely unsuccessful effort. Even in the early days of software development, when single programs were developed as projects, programmers were optimistic and estimating was a problem. There was no good way to convert the system or program requirements into an estimate of resources needed (even assuming that requirements had been adequately defined, which they often had not). A proposed program could be compared with a completed program, but in most cases statistics were not kept that could be used as input to a new estimating effort. Management always had another project in the bin, and programmers were moved to a new project as soon as possible. Considering the size of IT budgets, it is a bit surprising that, in some organizations, the move to require effective estimating techniques has only recently become a significant issue.

One of the bigger problems is controlling and accounting for requirements change (requirements creep) across the life cycle of a project. Capers Jones reports that the rate at which requirements change after their initial definition runs between 1 percent and more than 3 percent per month during the subsequent analysis, design, and coding phases. Equally as troublesome, software requirements are the source of about 20 percent of all software bugs or defects, and the source of more than 30 percent of really severe and difficult defects. The maximum amount of "creep" has been known to exceed 150 percent. "Since the requirements for more than 90% of all software projects change during development, creeping user requirements is numerically the most common problem of the software industry and should not be a surprise to anyone" [Jones, 1998].

Much of the problem is that requirements are often poorly defined; if the system is not fully understood, it cannot be estimated accurately. These inadequacies in requirements are exposed in the later stages of the delivery process and wreak havoc on the original estimates. A prerequisite for estimating is a comprehensive set of system requirements.

Requirements errors are often difficult to detect, because once the subsequent phases are reached, the requirements are the foundation for development and testing and it is assumed that they are correct. Right or wrong, they drive the design and construction phases, and testing simply verifies that what has been built is functioning correctly and will likely not detect missing or incorrect functionality. Not until user acceptance testing (UAT) will requirements errors be found.

So how can our estimates be adjusted to account for the requirements change? In the first place, system requirements creep must be controlled by improving the initial definition of the requirements. Once estimates are completed on the basis of the requirements, there must be a way of *detecting* requirements change and then *measuring* accurately the impact of the change on the original estimates. When estimates are based on user requirements, *adjusting* estimates is direct and natural.

The Standish Group has published statistics regarding 1,100 software projects, that show an average project duration of 222 percent of estimated duration. Although much of the problem lies in the definition of requirements, certainly some of it is attributable to the inaccuracy of the estimating techniques that are used. At times, a system is built very well and in minimum time but is still late and over budget due to an overly optimistic plan, poor estimating techniques, and/or a management-adjusted project schedule. These causes are particularly frustrating to a conscientious team that has done a very good job of managing the project and producing project deliverables.

10.2 Sources of Errors

Where do these estimating errors originate? Capers Jones, in his book *Estimating Software Costs* [1998], defines 12 classes of software estimation errors.

1. Metric errors: The most common errors in software estimating are those derived from the use of lines-of-code (LOC) metrics. The main problem with LOC metrics is the fact that more than half of all software effort is not directly related to source code, causing wide variance in estimates when different languages are used.

2. Scaling errors: A common source of estimating error is the assumption that data collected from small systems can be used for accurate estimation of large systems. Large systems perform more activities than do small systems, and the amounts of effort required for various kinds of work in a large system change significantly.

3. Executive and client errors: One of the most severe sources of software-estimation error centers around the fact that executives have the authority to reject valid estimates and shorten project schedules.

4. Sizing errors: Another common type of estimating error stems from underestimation of the sizes of deliverables. Examples are test cases, user procedures, and numbers of screens/windows.

5. Activity-selection errors: These errors result from omission of necessary work, such as user documentation, from the estimate.

6. Assignment-scope errors: Assignment-scope errors arise from overestimation of the quantity of work that the staff can handle, thus overloading staff members and further reducing their effectiveness.

7. Production-rate errors: These errors stem from including in the estimating algorithm inflated production rates such as coding rates and numbers of test-run pages per day.

8. Creeping user requirements: This type of error occurs when the estimate is not adjusted in response to changes and growth in the system requirements. Predicting and adjusting project estimates when requirements change is a standard function of modern cost-estimating techniques.

9. Critical path errors: "Software development is a complex net of hundreds of interlinked activities. A very common estimating problem is failure to identify the critical path through this network of activities, so that a delay in some key component or deliverable ripples downstream and lengthens the final delivery schedule" [Jones, 1998].

10. Staffing build-up errors: This type of error occurs when personnel are not available to join the development team as scheduled. This problem can be severe, because each day that a person is late delays the completion of the activity assigned to that person.

11. Technology adjustment errors: "The most subtle and complex of the sources of estimating errors are those dealing with adjusting the estimate to match the effects of various tools, languages, and methodologies" [Jones, 1998].

12. Special or unique situations: These errors include uncommon factors that do not occur with enough regularity to fit into standard estimating techniques.

Other errors can be encountered when a user group cannot or will not participate fully in the process of analysis and specification of requirements, delaying the process and increasing the risk of requirements errors. Finally, the interactions among teams, team members, and user groups involve many personalities and egos and can unpredictably disrupt the overall productivity of some individual teams.

The number and variety of errors indicate how involved and difficult the estimation of software projects can be and how easily estimates can contain significant errors if an organization fails to make an effort to implement modern, effective methods.

One might ask "Why estimate at all? Just build the system as effectively as possible and when it's done, it's done." In some cases, this would actually work. But many developers are not sufficiently disciplined to be productive without a target date that is close to realistic. Also, organizations must plan years ahead if they are to be competitive, and they must be able to plan software projects within reasonable timeframes.

10.3 Methods of Estimation

There are several techniques for estimating software projects. Capers Jones lists three general types of manual estimating methods [1998].

1. Project-level estimates using rules of thumb:
   - The oldest form of software cost estimation.
   - Still the most widely used.
   - Example: "Applications average 500 noncommentary lines of code per staff-month."

2. Phase-level estimates using ratios and percentages:
   - Also an old method of estimating.
   - Assign a total project size or a single phase size.
   - Apply percentages to the remaining phases; subsequent phases can be re-estimated as phases are completed and estimates become actual resources expended.
   - Example: Estimate that the requirements will take six weeks and that the other phases will take some fractions or multiples of that duration based on standard ratios.

3. Activity-level estimates using work-breakdown structures:
   - The most accurate of the manual methods.
   - Very time-consuming.
   - Difficult to modify.
   - Example: Break the project into activities (50 to 100, or more) and estimate each activity—for instance, design screen for "Fill Order."

However, with the dynamic nature of today's business and the complexity of its systems, many of them distributed, these methods can produce significant errors. Some estimates are projected to later phases on the basis of resources expended on early phases, whereas others estimate total effort based on an estimated system size in lines of code (LOC). Gaining in popularity is an estimating process based on "function points"—that is, a weighted sum of system inputs, outputs, files, interfaces, and database inquiries. This method is based on system requirements and is less dependent on physical system characteristics.

10.3.1 Lines of Code

The LOC method mentioned above applies coding productivity rates derived from an organization's history of software development or from published standards. The effort for non-code work such as testing and user procedures is added to the coding estimate. Tables presented in *Estimating Software Costs* [Jones, 1998] illustrate samples of the LOC-based rules of thumb for procedural languages using hours and months as the unit of work. Table 10.1 shows monthly work metrics.

As seen in Table 10.1, the percentage of effort allocated to non-code activities increases significantly as the size of the coding effort increases. These non-code tasks are rules of thumb based on history rather than on the requirements of the proposed system.

While LOC-based estimating rules of thumb served for many years, they are rapidly dropping from use because software technologies have changed so much that it is difficult, and even dangerous, to apply them under some conditions.

Table 10.1. LOC-based Monthly Work Metrics

Size of Program, LOC	Coding, LOC per Month	Coding Effort, Months	Testing Effort, %	Non-code Effort, %	Total Effort, Months	Net LOC per Month
1	2500	0.0004	10.00	10.00	0.0005	2,083
10	2250	0.0044	20.00	20.00	0.0062	1,607
100	2000	0.0500	40.00	40.00	0.0900	1,111
1,000	1750	0.5714	50.00	60.00	1.2000	833
10,000	1500	6.6667	75.00	80.00	17.0000	588
100,000	1200	83.3333	100.00	100.00	250.0000	400
1,000,000	1000	1000.0000	125.00	150.00	3750.0000	267

Usage of the LOC metric obviously assumes the existence of some kind of procedural programming language where programmers develop code using some combination of alphanumeric information, which is the way such languages as COBOL, C, FORTRAN, and hundreds of others operate.

However, the development of Visual Basic and its many competitors, such as Realizer, has changed the way many modern programs are developed. Although, these visual languages do have a procedural source code portion, quite a bit of the more complex kinds of "programming" are done using button controls, pull-down menus, visual worksheets, and reusable components. In other words, programming is being done without anything that can be identified as a *line of code* for measurement or estimation purposes. [Jones, 1998]

LOC for a given function not only is language-dependent but also can vary from programmer to programmer based on their skills and experience levels.

Another reason that the LOC metric is a questionable method for estimating large systems is that the programming ranks as only the fourth most expensive activity. The three higher activities—defect removal, production of paper documents, and meetings and communications—cannot be based on code [Jones, 1998].

10.3.2 Ratios and Percentages

Since much of the work effort is required by non-code activities, one method of estimating is based on the application of ratios and percentages to an overall project estimate.

The basic problem with ratio-based estimation is the false assumption that there are constant ratios between coding and other key activities, such as testing, project management, integration, and the like. In fact, the ratios vary significantly, based on four sets of independent variables:

1. The class of the application
2. The size of the application
3. The programming language or languages utilized
4. The presence or absence of reusable materials

The complexity of the interactions of these four sets of variables is why commercial software cost estimating tools contain hundreds of rules and adjustment factors. [Jones, 1998]

From tables presented in *Estimating Software Costs* [Jones, 1998], it can be seen that ratios based on software class vary from 60 percent coding for end-user projects to 18 percent for military projects. When compared by system size, coding ratios range from about 50 percent for small projects to 15 percent for larger projects.

With the newer visual languages being used today and the significant variance in ratios shown above, the use of ratios and percentages for estimating cannot deliver the accuracy needed for today's mission-critical systems.

10.4 Function Point Estimating

In the mid-1970s, IBM commissioned Allan J. Albrecht to find a code-independent method for software project estimating. The method, Function Point Analysis (FPA), was first published in 1979, and in 1986 the International Function Point Users Group (IFPUG) was established. IFPUG has released several versions of the *Function Point Counting Practices Manual,* with the latest, as of the writing of this text, being Release 4.1 in May 1999 [IFPUG, 1999]. The organization can be reached at:

International Function Point Users Group
Blendonview Office Park
5008-28 Pine Creek Drive
Westerville, OH 43081-4899
(614) 895-7130
(614) 895-3466 FAX
www.ifpug.org

Accurately estimating the effort of developing a software system has met with failure more often than success over the past few decades. Growth of membership in IFPUG and the growing number of function point organizations worldwide indicate that FPA is becoming widely accepted as the standard for measuring the size of a software project. Unlike the LOC metric, FPA is based on system requirements—that is, system functionality. Since it is based on the requirements of each system, FPA doesn't depend on retrofitting the experience (and the unique functionality) of another, past system to the proposed one. Each proposed system is judged on its own unique requirements.

With FPA, the numbers of inputs, outputs, inquiries, master files, and system interfaces are documented, weighted, and summed to produce an Unadjusted

Function Point Count (UFPC). The unadjusted count is then adjusted on the basis of general system characteristics. This method provides the following benefits.

- It can be used to analyze the impact of requirements change.

- It creates reasonably equivalent estimates when counted by different people at different times.

- Function points are based on system requirements and are therefore easier for the user to understand and verify.

Since FPA measures the size of a proposed information system on the basis of the conceptual requirements, it is therefore independent of technology. Regardless of the language used for development or the technology used for implementation, the number of function points remains constant. Because of its conceptual nature, FPA can be used to compare variations in physical components within an organization. It can also be used to measure changes in requirements by comparing the FPA elements at different phases of the life cycle. Many times, such changes in requirements can be a measure of how well requirements were defined in the first place and may reveal inadequacies in the requirements definition process.

FPA should be performed by trained and experienced analysts using the latest practices as found in the IFPUG *Function Point Counting Practices Manual*, Release 4.1. FPA should be part of an overall project plan.

10.4.1 Function Point Estimating Before Requirements

Typically, estimates will be expected for a proposed system before the requirements are even begun. Capers Jones, in *Estimating Software Costs*, describes a method for developing an early size estimate prior to completion of system requirements. This method generates a rough approximation of function point totals and has a high margin of error, "but it has the virtue of being usable before any other known form of sizing is possible" [Jones, 1998]. This method defines software projects in terms of scope, class, and type—information that is usually available early in the project life cycle. To use this method, the following three steps are performed (adapted from Jones, 1998).

1. Select the appropriate values from the lists of scope, class, and type factors. Choose only one value from each of the three lists.

Table 10.2.   Examples of Scope, Class, and Type Values

Scope	Class	Type
1. Subroutine	1. Individual software	1. Nonprocedural
2. Module	2. Shareware	2. Web applet
3. Reusable module	3. Academic software	3. Batch
4. Disposable prototype	4. Single location–internal	4. Interactive
5. Evolutionary prototype	5. Multilocation–internal	5. Interactive GUI
6. Standalone program	6. Contract project–civilian	6. Batch database
7. Component of system	7. Time sharing	7. Interactive database
8. Release of system	8. Military services	8. Client/server
9. New system	9. Internet	9. Mathematical
10. Compound system	10. Leased software	10. Systems
	11. Bundled software	11. Communications
	12. Marketed commercially	12. Process control
	13. Outsource contract	13. Trusted system
	14. Government contract	14. Embedded
	15. Military contract	15. Image processing
		16. Multimedia
		17. Robotics
		18. Artificial intelligence
		19. Neural net
		20. Hybrid: mixed

Table taken from *Estimating Software Costs* [Jones, 1998]

2. Add the three numeric values.

3. Raise the sum to the power 2.35.

For example, if you are building a standalone, client/server program to be implemented at a single internal site, you would likely select from Table 10.2 as follows.

Scope = 6
Class = 4
Type = 8
Sum = 18

Raising 18 to the power 2.35 produces a system size estimate of 891 function points (13–26 work hours per function point approximates normal performance [Jones, 1998]). This will allow some early sizing but will be discarded when requirements are defined and used for FPA. Other sizing techniques that can be used before requirements are completed can be found in *Estimating Software Costs* [Jones, 1998, page 188].

10.4.2 Function Point Estimating Based on Requirements

The first time in the development process when enough information is available for an accurate estimate is following the definition of system requirements. Of course, an estimate at this time depends on the accuracy of the requirements analysis and specification effort. FPA is based on the complexity of the proposed system functions, and so a single complex function can result in as many function points as two or three simpler functions.

Because FPA is based on a user perspective of the system and on a conceptual view of the system, it is therefore technology-independent. This allows for more effective user verification of the estimation results and is not affected by decisions such as choosing the development language. It should also be noted that formal training and even certification in the use of FPA is recommended to ensure the highest degree of accuracy. A good method used poorly by untrained personnel will likely yield poor, inaccurate results.

Estimating with function points has two major components: a Function Point Count (FPC) based on system functionality, and an adjustment factor based on general system characteristics. The following outline shows component decomposition.

Function Point Count (FPC)
  Transaction components:
    - External Inputs (EIs)
    - External Outputs (EOs)
    - External Inquiries (EQs)
  Data components:
    - Internal Logical Files (ILFs)
    - External Interface Files (EIFs)
Adjustment factor
  14 General System Characteristics (GSCs)

When the complexity values have been determined, they are weighted as shown in Table 10.3.

Unadjusted Function Points—Component Identification

To begin the process of estimating system size using FPCs, an Unadjusted Function Point Count (UFPC) is calculated. Five system components must be identified, and these components fall into two categories—transaction and data—based on a set of predefined rules. For each of the *transaction types,* the process must be the smallest unit of activity that is meaningful to the end user in the business. This process must be self-contained and must leave the business of the application being counted in a consistent state. For the transactional function types to be counted, all of the following rules must apply.

Table 10.3.   System Component Complexity Weights

	Complexity		
Type of Component	Low	Average	High
External Inputs	3	4	6
External Outputs	4	5	7
External Inquiries	3	4	6
Internal Logical Files	7	10	15
External Interface Files	5	7	10

1. External Inputs (EIs): Data that comes from an external agent and crosses the system boundary from outside to inside.
   - The data is received from outside the application boundary (examples: keyboard entry, barcode reader).
   - The data is used to maintain an ILF.
   - For the identified process, one of the following two rules must apply:
     - The processing logic is unique with respect to other external inputs to the application.
     - The identified data elements are different from other external inputs for the application.

2. External Outputs (EOs): Data that is generated by the system and crosses the system boundary from inside to outside.
   - The process sends data or control information external to the application's boundary (examples: reports, screens, files to other applications).
   - The data or control information is sent through an elementary process of the application.
   - For the identified process, one of the following two rules must apply:
     - The processing logic is unique with respect to other external outputs from the application.
     - The identified data elements are different from other external outputs for the application.

3. External Inquiries (EQs): Data passes from an external agent into the system and results in data retrieval and generation of an external output. No internal files are updated.
   - An input request enters the application boundary (example: a request to view all sales for a specified date).
   - Output results exit the application boundary.
   - Data is retrieved.
   - The retrieved data does not contain derived data.
   - The input request and output results together make up a process that is the smallest unit of activity that is meaningful to the end user in the business.
   - The processing does not update an ILF.
   - For the identified process, one of the following two rules must apply:
     - The processing logic on the input or output side is unique with respect to other external inquiries to the application.

- The data elements making up the input or output side are different from other external inquiries to the application.

Data function types represent the functionality provided to the user to meet internal and external data requirements. Data function types are defined as ILFs and EIFs.

The term *file* here is not meant in the traditional data processing sense. In this case, file refers to a logically related group of data, such as a normalized conceptual entity, and not the physical implementation of that group of data. For each of the data types to be counted, all of the associated rules must apply.

4. Internal Logical Files (ILFs): A group of logically related data that resides within the boundary of the proposed system and is maintained by the proposed system.
   - The group of data or control information is a logical, or user-identifiable, group of data that fulfills specific user requirements (examples: an entity from the conceptual data model such as Parts or Orders).
   - The group of data is maintained within the application boundary.
   - The group of data is modified, or maintained, through an elementary process of the application.
   - The identified group of data has not been counted as an EIF for the application.

5. External Interface Files (EIFs): A group of logically related data that resides outside the boundaries of the proposed system and is maintained by another application. It is used by the proposed system for reference purposes only.
   - The group of data or control information is a logical, or user-identifiable, group of data that fulfills specific user requirements.
   - The group of data is referenced by, and external to, the application being counted.
   - The group of data is not maintained by the application being counted.
   - The group of data is counted as an ILF for at least one other application.
   - The identified group of data has not been counted as an ILF for the application.

Unadjusted Function Points—Complexity Ranking

Once all of the components of the system have been identified and classified, their complexity must be ranked as low, average, or high (see Tables 10.4. and 10.5). The ranking for EIs, EOs, and EQs is based on:

Table 10.4.   External Inputs (EIs)

Record Element Types	Data Element Types		
	1–4	5–15	Greater than 15
Less than 2	Low	Low	Average
2	Low	Average	High
Greater than 2	Average	High	High

- The number of record element types, where a record element type is a sub-group of data elements within a file (example: commercial or individual order data).

- The number of data element types, where a data element type is a data attribute, a column in a relational table, or a field in a record.

For inquiries, the input side is ranked using the EIs in Table 10.4 and the output side is ranked using the EOs in Table 10.5. Rank the External Inquiry (EQ) equal to the higher of the input and output rankings. When ranking ILFs and EIFs, the number of data elements and the number of referenced and updated files are used to determine a ranking of low, average, or high and are based on the number of record element types and the number of data element types (see Tables

Table 10.5.   External Outputs (EOs)

Record Element Types	Data Element Types		
	1–5	6–19	Greater than 19
Less than 2	Low	Low	Average
2 or 3	Low	Average	High
Greater than 3	Average	High	High

Table 10.6.   Internal Logical Files (ILFs)

Record Element Types	Data Element Types		
	1–19	20–50	Greater than 50
1	Low	Low	Average
2–5	Low	Average	High
Greater than 5	Average	High	High

10.6 and 10.7). When the complexity values have been determined, weighted subtotals and a grand total are calculated as shown in Table 10.8.

Value Adjustment Factor

Now that the total UFPC has been determined, a Value Adjustment Factor (VAF) is generated on the basis of 14 IFPUG General System Characteristics (GSCs) [IFPUG, 1994]. Other methods, such as British Mark II and the SPR feature point metric, apply a different set of adjustments.

The possible values of each characteristic is zero to five, where zero is no influence on the complexity of the system and five is the strongest influence. Table 10.9 shows the assignment of adjustment weights [Jones 1998].

Table 10.7.   External Interface Files (EIFs)

Record Element Types	Data Element Types		
	1–19	20–50	Greater than 50
1	Low	Low	Average
2–5	Low	Average	High
Greater than 5	Average	High	High

Table 10.8.   Weighted Component Complexity Totals

Type of Component	Complexity Low	Complexity Average	Complexity High	Sub-total
External Inputs	____ × 3 = ____	____ × 4 = ____	____ × 6 = ____	____
External Outputs	____ × 4 = ____	____ × 5 = ____	____ × 7 = ____	____
External Inquiries	____ × 3 = ____	____ × 4 = ____	____ × 6 = ____	____
Internal Logical Files	____ × 7 = ____	____ × 10 = ____	____ × 15 = ____	____
External Interface Files	____ × 5 = ____	____ × 7 = ____	____ × 10 = ____	____
			Total Unadjusted Function Point Count (UFPC)	____

Each general characteristic must be evaluated on the basis of its influence on the complexity of the proposed system. It is easy to see that there is a significant amount of subjectivity involved with those assignments.

The variations in complexity adjustments for function point totals have been a troublesome and contentious aspect of function point analysis. Indeed, the ambiguity and partial subjectivity of the adjustments have led several researchers to assert that the counts might be more accurate if the

Table 10.9.   Component Complexity Weights

0	Not present or no influence at all
1	Minor influence
2	Moderate influence
3	Average influence
4	Significant influence
5	Strong, pervasive influence

complexity adjustments were dispensed with and not even used at all. [Jones, 1998]

The GSCs are

1. Data communications
2. Distributed data processing
3. Performance
4. Heavily used configuration
5. Transaction rate
6. Online data entry
7. End-user efficiency
8. Online update
9. Complex processing
10. Reusability
11. Installation ease
12. Operational ease
13. Multiple sites
14. Facilitate change

For each GSC, the IFPUG manual includes guidelines for determining the degree of influence. The following sections in this chapter are devoted to those guidelines.

Guidelines for Determining Degrees of Influence

This section presents an example of the guidelines for determining the degree of influence for each GSC as described in the IFPUG *Function Point Counting Practices Manual,* Release 4.0. The remaining 13 tables can be found in Appendix C.

The weights in the tables are guides only. A judgment must be made to determine which degree of influence most closely applies to the application under consideration.

Data Communications: The *data* and *control* information used in the application are sent or received over communications facilities. Terminals connected locally to the control unit are considered to use communications facilities. Protocol is a set of conventions that permit the transfer or exchange of information between two systems or devices. All data communications links require some type of protocol (see Table 10.10).

Table 10.10.   Data Communications Degree of Influence

Score as	Descriptions to Determine Degree of Influence
0	Application is pure batch processing or a standalone PC.
1	Application is batch but has remote data entry *or* remote printing.
2	Application is batch but has remote data entry *and* remote printing.
3	Application includes online data collection or TP (teleprocessing) front end to a batch process or query system.
4	Application is more than a front end but supports only one type of TP communications protocol.
5	Application is more than a front end and supports more than one type of TP communications protocol.

Value Adjustment Factor Calculation

When each of the GSCs has been assigned its degree of influence, they are summed to arrive at the total General System Degree of Influence (GSDI). This sum is then adjusted to arrive at the VAF using the following equation.

$$VAF = 0.65 + (0.01 \times GSDI)$$

The value of the VAF can vary from 0.65, when the total complexity weight is zero, to 1.35, when the total complexity weight is 70 (all 5's). The VAF is an adjustment factor that is applied to the Function Point Count (FPC) derived from the five original system components and represents the influence on system size of the GSCs.

$$FPC = UFPC \times VAF$$

The final FPC is a measure of the size of the proposed system considering five system components and adjusted by a factor derived from GSCs. It is based on the conceptual system requirements.

10.4.3 IFPUG Abbreviated Example

Let's work through an abbreviated example. A simple transaction processing system with a database and some on-line data retrieval can be represented by the following components. A more detailed example follows in Chapter 11.

EI = 5 (1 simple, 3 average, 1 complex)
EO = 13 (10 simple, 3 complex)
EQ = 7 (7 average)
ILF = 7 (5 simple, 1 average, 1 complex)
EIF = 3 (1 simple, 1 average, 1 complex)

Applying the system component complexity values (boldface to left of equal sign) to the complexity weights produces the results shown in Table 10.11. The total UFPC is 192. Next, the adjustment factor from the GSCs must be applied (using the IFPUG list) (see Table 10.12). These complexity values are based on a typical project for the system described above. This adjustment factor total is divided by 100 and then added to 0.65. The final adjusted FPC is calculated as follows.

$$VAF = 0.65 + (0.01 \times 33) = 0.98$$
$$FPC = UFPC \times VAF = 192 \times 0.98 = 188 \text{ function points}$$

Using an approximation of 130 work hours per month and the normal productivity range (13 to 26 work hours per function point), the following application can be made to the function points calculated in the example above.

Table 10.11.   Unadjusted Function Point Calculation

Type of Component	Complexity Low	Complexity Average	Complexity High	Total
External Inputs	$1 \times 3 = 3$	$3 \times 4 = 12$	$1 \times 6 = 6$	21
External Outputs	$10 \times 4 = 40$		$3 \times 7 = 21$	61
External Inquiries		$7 \times 4 = 28$		28
Internal Logical Files	$5 \times 7 = 35$	$1 \times 10 = 10$	$1 \times 15 = 15$	60
External Interface Files	$1 \times 5 = 5$	$1 \times 7 = 7$	$1 \times 10 = 10$	22
			Total Unadjusted Function Point Count (UFPC)	192

Table 10.12.   GSC Adjustment Factors

Data communications	1	Online update	3
Distributed functions	1	Complex processing	1
Performance goals	2	Reusability	1
Configuration usage	3	Installation ease	3
Transaction rates	3	Operational ease	2
Online data entry	4	Multiple-site usage	0
End-user efficiency	4	Facilitate change	5
		Total adjustment factor	33

Lower end of normal range (two variations of calculations):

1. 188 function points × 13 work hours per function point = *2,444 work hours required*
2. 188 function points/10 function points per staff-month = 18.8 staff-months
   18.8 staff-months × 130 work hours per staff-month = *2,444 required work hours*

Upper end of normal range (two variations of calculations):

1. 188 function points × 26 work hours per function point = *4,888 work hours required*
2. 188 function points/5 function points per staff-month = 37.6 staff-months
   37.6 staff-months × 130 work hours per staff-month = *4,888 required work hours*

10.4.4 The SPR Method

One alternative to the IFPUG method comes from Software Productivity Research, Inc. (SPR) in Burlington, Massachusetts. The SPR method differs in the way in which the complexity adjustment multiplier is determined and, in many cases, achieves results that are similar to the IFPUG method. For normal forward function point calculations, SPR uses only two adjustment factors compared to the 14 of the IFPUG method. The SPR method was designed to be used in a rule-based expert system while the IFPUG method was intended to generate manual counts and to be used by human function point specialists.

SPR function point complexity adjustment uses the sum of *problem complexity* and *data complexity* scores. Like the IFPUG method, SPR complexity adjustments utilize a five-point weighting scale. Tables 10.13 and 10.14 illustrate the guidelines for determining the complexity factor.

Once the two complexity factors are determined, their sum is used to reference Table 10.15 to arrive at an adjustment multiplier. For example, complexity values of 3 and 4 (sum 7) return an adjustment multiplier of 1.1. Note that from Table 10.15, the minimum and maximum multipliers are 0.5 and 1.5, compared with 0.65 and 1.35 for IFPUG.

10.4.5 SPR Abbreviated Example

If we apply the SPR method to the preceding example, the following results are achieved.

Problem complexity for this type of system is not a major factor since most processing is involved with updating of database tables and retrieval of data for reporting purposes. It will be assumed that some simple calculations might have to be made for a few of the screen or report components.

Problem complexity = 1

Since this is a typical database application, data complexity will be higher than the problem complexity. Most business applications that have both online transaction processing and decision support components are not especially complex. They deal with data tables of average complexity and size that have fairly normal relationships. With this in mind, a complexity factor of 3 was chosen for this example. The number of associative tables involved should be considered here since they tend to require more complex processing owing to multiple-attribute

Table 10.13. Problem Complexity

1	All simple algorithms and simple calculations
2	Majority of simple algorithms and simple calculations
3	Algorithms and calculations of average complexity
4	Some difficult or complex algorithms or calculations
5	Many difficult algorithms and complex calculations

Table 10.14. Data Complexity

1 Simple data with few elements and relationships
2 Numerous variable and constant data items, but simple relationship
3 Average complexity with multiple files, fields, and data relationships
4 Complex file structures and complex data relationships
5 Very complex file structures and very complex data relationships

keys. In this case, however, they will not likely kick the data complexity value up from 3 to 4.

Data complexity = 3

Using the sum of 4 to reference the SPR complexity adjustment in Table 10.15, a multiplier of 0.8 is obtained and results in a final FPC of 154.

$$FPC = UFPC \times VAF = 192 \times 0.8 = 153.6 \text{ function points}$$

Table 10.15. Complexity Adjustment Multiplier

Sum of Problem and Data Complexity	Adjustment Multiplier
1	0.5
2	0.6
3	0.7
4	0.8
5	0.9
6	1.0
7	1.1
8	1.2
9	1.3
10	1.4
11	1.5

10.5 Application of Function Point Count

The next question might be "What do we do with the FPC?" In addition to sizing a proposed system, function points can be used to compare productivity and defect rates with software standards. Capers Jones lists the following generic ranges of software productivity levels [1998]:

- Projects of less than 5 function points per staff-month (more than 26 work hours per function point) have productivity levels that are below U.S. averages for all software projects.

- Projects between 5 and 10 function points per staff-month (13 to 26 work hours per function point) approximate the normal range of productivity for U.S. software projects.

- Projects between 10 and 20 function points per staff-month (7 to 13 work hours per function point) have productivity levels that are higher than U.S. averages for software projects.

- Projects above 20 function points per staff-month (7 work hours per function point) have productivity levels that are significantly higher than U.S. averages for software projects.

This information can vary with the class of system being considered and also with the size of the application. "Small projects of less than 100 function points in size often top 20 function points per staff month, but for larger projects above 1,000 function points in size such results are extremely rare" [Jones, 1998]. Jones also offers the following defect rates when using function point metrics.

- A delivered defect rate of more than 1.50 bugs per function point is very bad.

- A delivered defect rate of less than 0.75 bug per function point is normal.

- A delivered defect rate of less than 0.10 bug per function point is very good.

Function points can be used to measure and compare requirements "creep" by calculating the function points for each new system requirement. The percentage of the total project estimate that each new requirement represents can give project managers an idea of the impact that the new requirement will have on the entire development effort. They can then bargain for additional resources as necessary. Some additional benefits of function point metrics are noted by Jones [1998].

- Function points stay constant regardless of the programming languages used.

- Function points are a good choice for full-life-cycle analysis.

- Function points are a good choice for software reuse analysis.

- Function points are a good choice for object-oriented economic studies.

- Function points are supported by many software cost estimating tools.

- Function points can be mathematically converted into logical code statements for many languages.

The main weaknesses of function point metrics are as follows [Jones, 1998].

- Accurate counting requires certified function point specialists.

- Function point counting can be time-consuming and expensive.

- Function point counting automation is of unknown accuracy.

- Function point counts are erratic for projects below 15 function points in size.

- Function point variations have no conversion rules to IFPUG function points.

- Many function point variations have no backfiring conversion rules.

- General system complexity adjustments tend to be ambiguous and subjective.

10.6 Automated Estimating Tools

There are currently about 50 commercial software estimating tools available. Jones describes nearly 60 major features of the family of commercial software estimating tools, but most tools contain at least the basic features shown below [Jones, 1998].

- On-board knowledge base of more than 1,000 projects

- Sizing logic for specifications, source code, and test cases

- Support for software process assessment questions

- Phase-level or activity-level effort, cost, and schedule estimation

- Support for both function point metrics and the older lines-of-code (LOC) metrics

- Support for conversion between lines of code and function points

- Quality and reliability estimation, as well as cost and schedule estimation

- Interfaces to project management tools

- Support for dozens of standard development methods

- Customization support for unique development methods

As often seems to be the case, these tools may have exceeded the functionality necessary to do basic project estimating. As tool companies battle for market share, they tend to add functions to make their offerings more attractive and distinctive. But is a software package even necessary? The answer is no, but as with many other software development tasks, it may be more productive and accurate to use one. On the other hand, if the complexity of the tool requires an excessive amount of resources to learn and use, it is unlikely that it will bring much of an advantage to the estimation effort or be used consistently.

There are about 50 software-estimating tools available in the United States. The following list is representative of those tools [Jones, 1998].

- Adaptive Estimating Model (AEM)

- Before You Leap (BYL)

- Bridge Modeler

- CHECKPOINT

- COCOMO

- COCOMO II

- CoCoPro

- COSTMODELER

- COSTMODL

- COSTAR

- COSTEXPERT

- ESTIMACS

- GECOMO

- KnowledgePlan

- MicroMan

- PRICE-S

- ProQMS

- REVIC

- SASET

- SOFTCALC

- SOFTCOST

- SEER

- SLIM

- SPQR/20

With so many tools on the market and an ever-increasing need for accurate software estimates, where is the world of software estimation headed?

10.7 The Future of Function Point Analysis

Organizations tend to be reluctant to implement project metrics even though project estimation remains a major problem. Since fewer than 9 percent of companies in the United States use metrics to measure and monitor software development, it's not surprising that on a list of 19 issues that included recruitment, productivity, and project management, metrics rated dead last.

However, the function point method of software project estimation continues to grow in popularity. The International Function Point User Group (IFPUG) has grown from 100 members in 1987 to nearly 600 members in 1994. From 1988 until 1994, conference attendance increased from 125 to 315.

While some of the function point techniques continue to be largely subjective, there is hope that continued research will move FPA toward a more scientific method. It seems that having user requirements as a foundation for function points is a solid one. As the method improves, more and more organizations will likely get on board.

10.8 Integration of Events and Function Points

An event-driven approach to the definition of requirements offers many benefits to the use of function points for software project estimating. Since function points are determined from system functionality from the users' perspective and events are a partitioning of user real-world requirements, the two methods dovetail to form a natural estimating technique. The event models reveal most of the components needed to make a function point estimate. Since the system is partitioned by responses to events, FPCs can be made event by event and can evolve as the requirements are defined. Incremental releases of the system as well as the total system effort can be estimated.

Because event responses have very low coupling, they can be taken vertically through the delivery process (requirements, design, construction) while other event responses are being investigated and defined. FPA can be applied to each individual event response and totaled to determine the size of a system release.

The diagram that provides the most value is the Event Diagram (event DFD). These diagrams, along with the data model, typically contain the following system components that relate directly to the FPC.

- Input data flows

- Output data flows

- Updates to files (create, update, delete)

- File reads

- Number of files involved

- Structure of files involved

- Number of external agent interfaces

- Interfaces to other systems

- Process business rules

- Attributes in an input data flow

- Attributes in an output data flow

- Transaction rates along data flows

- Performance goals for each event response

When used with the data model (Entity Relationship Diagram, or ERD), 10 of the 19 IFPUG components (5 system components plus 14 GSCs) are provided. Other function point elements are found in the geographic matrix and the CRUD matrix (Event-Entity matrix). Although they can be identified at the Event Diagram level, interfaces to external agents and to other systems are often more easily identified in a Context Diagram. This diagram, however, often does not provide sufficient detail for the function point counting.

Context Diagram

- Interfaces to external users

- Interfaces to other systems

Geographic matrix

- Data communications

- Distributed functions

- Multiple-site usage

Event-Entity (CRUD) matrix

- Type of file access (create, read, update, delete)

- Frequency of file access

- Complexity of file access (file type and access type); for example, associative entities typically involve more complex processing than other entity types

An event approach to defining system requirements provides most of the artifacts needed for function point counting. The mapping of the 19 IFPUG function point factors to the requirements models are summarized in Table 10.16. In some cases, the models contain only part of the information required for function point counting.

Table 10.16.   Function Point Components–Requirements Models Matrix

Function Point Components	Data Model	Event Diagram	Event-Entity Matrix	Geographic Matrix	Context Diagram
External Inputs		X			
External Outputs		X			
External Inquiries		X			
Internal Logical Files	X	X	X		
External Interface Files		X			X
Data Communications				X	
Distributed Functions				X	
Performance Goals		X			
Configuration Usage					
Transaction Rates		X			
Online Data Entry		X			
End-user Efficiency					
Online Update		X	X		
Complex Processing		X	X		
Reusability					
Installation Ease					
Operational Ease					
Multiple-site Usage				X	
Facilitate Change					

CHAPTER ELEVEN

Function Point Example

- 11.1 **Data Function Types**
- 11.2 **Transactional Function Types**
- 11.3 **General System Characteristics**
- 11.4 **Adjustment to Function Points**
- 11.5 **Example Summary**

An extended version of the example of the Cyber Order System used in Part II of this book will be used for illustrating the counting of function points as part of an event-driven strategy. It breaks down into the five event responses listed in Table 11.1.

Table 11.1.   Cyber Order System Event Responses

Business Event	Event Response
1. Customer places order	Fill order (transaction processing)
2. Customer returns item	Return item (transaction processing)
3. Candidate requests customer status	Add customer (transaction processing)
5. Customer inquires about item availability	Produce item availability (inquiry)
6. Time to generate daily sales report	Generate daily sales report (report)

The function point strategy is composed of two major parts. One part focuses on the individual event responses and their contribution to an Unadjusted Function Point Count (UFPC). The second part examines General System Characteristics (GSCs) and adjusts the UFPC by a factor ranging from 0.65 to 1.35.

The first step will be to count the five component types for each event response. The total UFPC will be the sum of the individual event-response counts. The material in this chapter will consider event responses 1, 2, 3, 5, and 6. To limit the redundancy in the following example, only two transaction event responses (responses 1 and 2) and one query event response (response 5) will actually use the models in the count determination. Event responses 3 and 6 follow along the same patterns.

The matrix shown in Table 11.2 maps the Cyber Order System event responses and data model to the function point components.

Table 11.3 shows the Unadjusted Function Points. (Boldface values to the right of the equal sign represent variable data; boldface values to the left of the equal sign represent component complexity values.) The example will evolve to illustrate how each value was determined.

Table 11.2.   Cyber Order System Function Point Components

Event Response/ Data Model	EI	EO	EQ	ILF	EIF
Fill order	X	X			
Return item	X	X			
Add customer	X	X			
Produce item availability			X		X
Generate daily sales report			X		
Data Model				X	

EI = External Inputs, EO = External Outputs, EQ = External Inquiries, ILF = Internal Logical Files, EIF = External Interface Files

Table 11.3. Cyber Order System Unadjusted Function Points

Type of Component	Complexity Low	Complexity Average	Complexity High	Total
External Inputs		$1 \times 4 = 4$	$2 \times 6 = 12$	**16**
External Outputs	$5 \times 4 = 20$	$3 \times 5 = 15$		**35**
External Inquiries	$2 \times 3 = 6$		$1 \times 6 = 6$	**12**
Internal Logical Files	$5 \times 7 = 35$			**35**
External Interface Files	$2 \times 5 = 10$			**10**
			Total Unadjusted Function Point Count (UFPC)	**108**

11.1 Data Function Types

11.1.1 External Interface Files

To begin with, the external system interfaces can be examined and the complexity documented as high, average, or low. From the Context Diagram (Figure 11.1), it can be determined that the system under study reads a purchasing database to obtain vendor information. The detail of this transaction can be examined using the DFD of the event response that is responsible for the access—in this case, *Produce Item Availability.* Using information from this diagram and the IFPUG guidelines, two low-complexity files (Vendor Item and Vendor Order) are assigned (each a single record element type and less than 20 data elements).

External Interface Files	$2 \times 5 = 10$	**10**

11.1.2 Internal Logical Files

Next, values for the Internal Logical Files (ILFs) can be determined from the data model (Figure 11.2). The fundamental entities (Customer and Item) along with the associative and attributive entities (Credit History and Ordered Item) have one record element type and fewer than 20 data elements. These four entities will

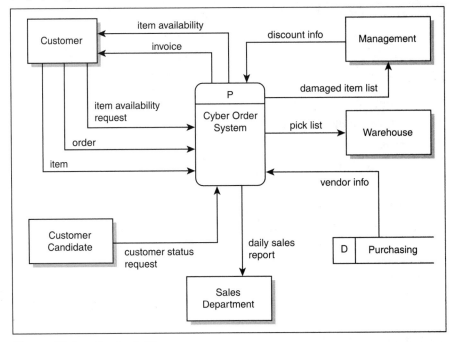

Figure 11.1   Context Diagram

contribute four low-complexity ILFs. The Order entity and its two subtypes (Commercial and Individual) have three record element types and fewer than 20 data elements. They will count as one low-complexity file.

Internal Logical Files	$5 \times 7 = 35$	**35**

11.2 Transactional Function Types

The next three complexity factors can be determined from each of the event diagrams and then summed into the Unadjusted Function Points Table. Although there are five events in this example, only three, as mentioned earlier, will be illustrated with DFDs. These event responses represent transaction processing (*Fill Order* and *Return Item*) and an inquiry *(Produce Item Availability)*. The corresponding event-response models are shown in Figures 11.3 through 11.5.

Use of the CRUD matrix, shown in Table 11.4, is of value during consideration of these system components because it provides understanding of the way in which the files are processed. Note from the matrix in Table 11.4 that the

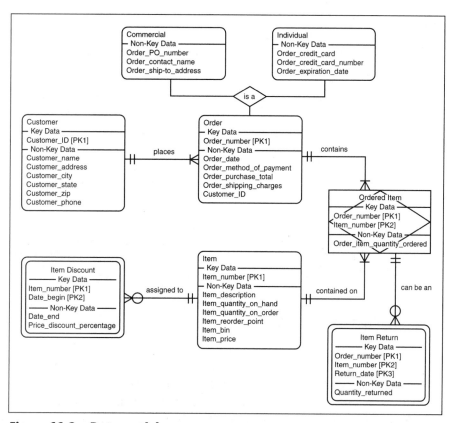

Figure 11.2 Data model

Table 11.4. Entity/Event Response Table (CRUD Matrix)

Event Response	Customer	Item Discount	Item	Order	Ordered Item
Fill order	R	R	RU	C	C
Process return	R		RU	R	R
Add customer	RC				
Record discount information		CU	R		
Produce item availability	R		R		
Generate daily sales report	R			R	R

C = Create, R = Read, U = Update

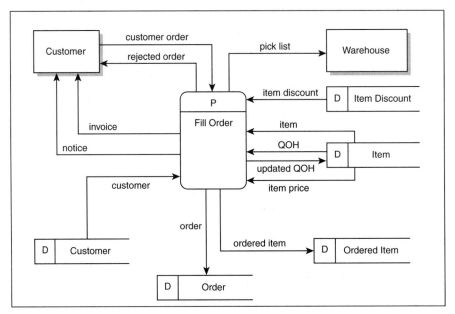

Figure 11.3   Fill Order

associative entity (Ordered Item) is created by only one event response for this release of the system. This is significant since associative entities tend to require more complex processing. Also note that two of the event responses (Fill Order and Process Return) access at least four entities, with one performing one update and the other performing two creates and one update (see Figures 11.3 through 11.5).

Fill Order—Specification
Validate order
    customer on file
    valid date not later than current date
    not null: PO, contact name, credit card information
    {item on file
    numeric quantity }
If invalid, reject for re-entry
Generate next order number

For each valid item
    Using valid order

        If quantity on hand less than quantity ordered

           generate notice

        End If

    Using valid order

        get item information (Item)

        add to pick list

    Using valid order

        get QOH (Item)

        update QOH

    Using valid order

        get item price (Item)

        get price discount percentage by order date (Item Discount)

        calculate charges (BR 1)

    Using valid order and charges

        generate ordered item (Ordered Item)

End For

BR 1: ((((Item price * Item price discount)*quantity ordered)*tax rate)

Using order number

    generate pick list

Using valid order and charges

    generate order (Order)

Using valid order and charges

    get customer information (Customer)

    generate invoice

Customer order =	Ship-to address =	Pick list =
customer ID	recipient name	order number
date order sent	street address	{item number
ship-to address	city	item description
PO number	state	item bin
contact name	zip	quantity ordered}
credit card		
{item number	Credit card =	
description of item	credit card name	
quantity ordered	credit card number	
catalog price}	credit card expiration date	

Notice =
    order number
    customer ID
    customer phone
    date order sent
    item number
    item description
    order item quantity ordered

Invoice =
    customer ID
    customer name
    ship-to address
    {item number
    item description
    order item quantity ordered
    item price}

Performance requirements: response time of less than three seconds

Transaction rates: 300 orders per hour

Return Item—Specification

Validate return
    order on file
    valid order date not later than current date
    {item on file
    instance exists on Ordered Item}
If invalid, reject for re-entry

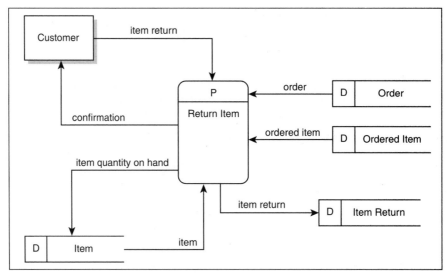

Figure 11.4   Return Item

For each valid item

    Using valid order and valid item

        get order information (Order)

        get ordered item (Ordered Item)

        get item information (Item)

        present information

    Using valid item

        update QOH (BR 1)

    Using valid order item

        update order_item_quantity_ordered with zero

        create item return (Item Return)

End For

Generate confirmation

BR 1: updated QOH = QOH + returned nondefect quantity

Item return =   Confirmation =

    order number   current date

    order date   {item description

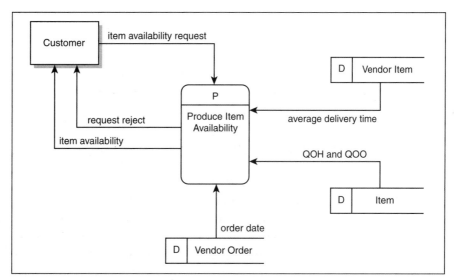

Figure 11.5   Produce Item Availability

{item number   quantity returned}

quantity returned}

Produce Item Availability–Specification

Begin process

    Validate request

      item on file

    If invalid, reject for re-entry

    Get item availability information (Item)

    Get vendor information*

    Get vendor order information*

    Calculate expected order arrival date (BR1)

    Generate item availability

End Process

BR1: expected order arrival date = order date + vendor average delivery time (in days)

*These tables were not included in the original running example in Chapters 5 through 9.

Item availability request =   Item availability =

    item number   item number

                              item description

                                item quantity on hand

                                item quantity on order

                                expected order arrival date

11.2.1 External Inputs

External Inputs (EIs) are data flows that cross the system boundary from outside to inside (DFD data flows from an external agent to the process). Any data flow from an external agent into the system will be counted. In the preceding *Fill Order* event response, *customer order* is the only input flow. An examination of the contents of the flow in the specification reveals six attributes one time and four attributes as a repeating group (curly brackets). During the processing of the inputs, four files are referenced or updated. This will be ranked as *high* complexity.

External Inputs	$1 \times 6 = 6$

In the *Return Item* event response, *item return* is the only input flow. An examination of the contents of this flow in the specification reveals two attributes and a repeating group of two attributes. Three files are referenced and/or updated, so this will be ranked as *high* complexity.

External Inputs		$1 \times 6 = 6$

The *Add Customer* response has one request input flow (all customer attributes), reads two files, and creates an instance of one file. Therefore, this event response contributes one average external input to complete the table row,· as shown below. Keep in mind that one of the event responses is a query and one is a temporal report and that these responses will be considered separately. Only three are being counted at this point and are reflected in this table fragment.

External Inputs	$1 \times 4 = 4$	$2 \times 6 = 12$	16

11.2.2 External Outputs

External Outputs (EOs) are data flows that cross the system boundary from inside to outside (DFD data flows from the process to an external agent). Any data flow from the system to an external agent will be counted. In the *Fill Order* event response, there are five output flows. An examination of the contents of the data flows in the specification reveals the following data structures. Their complexity will be ranked as shown in Table 11.5.

External Outputs	$2 \times 4 = 8$	$3 \times 5 = 15$

In the *Return Item* event response, *item return reject* (not shown on the DFD but described in the pseudocode) and *confirmation* are the only output flows. An examination of the contents of these flows in the specification reveals the data structures shown in Table 11.6. They will both be ranked as *low* complexity.

External Outputs	$2 \times 4 = 8$

By now you have probably disagreed with some of the rankings. Some would feel it is better to be high than low. Either way, it is easy to see the subjectivity of the method.

The other event response *(Add Customer)* contributes one low EO to complete the table row as shown below. Only three are being counted at this point and are shown in this table fragment.

External Outputs	$5 \times 4 = 20$	$3 \times 5 = 15$	35

Table 11.5. *Fill Order* **External Outputs**

Data Flow	Data Structure	RET	Complexity Rating
rejected order	(customer order) + message	1	low
rejected item	(item number, quantity ordered) + message	1	low
notice	7 attributes	2	average
invoice	3 attributes + 4 repeating attributes*	2	average
pick list	1 attribute + 4 repeating attributes*	2	average

*Repeating items for large orders could give this item a "high" ranking.
RET = Record Element Type

Note: *Rejected Item* is part of the *Rejected Order* data flow and is shown as a repeating group in the pseudocode {item on file, numeric quantity}.

11.2.3 External Inquiries

External Inquiries (EQs) represent elementary processes where (1) data passes from an external agent into the system and results in data retrieval and generation of an external output, and (2) reporting functions are temporal in nature. No internal files are updated. These functions are counted separately and are not included in the EI or EO counts. For this example, *Produce Item Availability* and *Generate Daily Sales Report* will qualify as EQs.

Any data flows to or from an external agent will be counted as in the EI and EO counts above, and then the higher of the two will be used for the inquiry

Table 11.6. *Return Item* **External Outputs**

Data Flow	Data Structure	RET	Complexity Rating
item return reject	2 attributes + message	3	low
confirmation	1 attribute + 2 repeating attributes	1	low

RET = Record Element Type

Table 11.7. *Produce Item Availability* **External Inquiry**

Data Flow	Data Structure	RET	Complexity Rating
item availability request	1 attribute	1	low
availability request reject	1 attribute + message	1	low
item availability	5 attributes	3	low

RET = Record Element Type

count. In the *Produce Item Availability* event response, there is one input flow, two output flows, and three table reads. An examination of the contents of the data flows in the specification reveals the following data structures. Their complexity will be ranked as shown in Table 11.7. This event response will contribute two low outputs since both the input and the output flows have low complexity.

External Inquiries	$2 \times 3 = 6$

The reporting event response *(Generate Daily Sales Report)* accesses five record types along with seven data elements and contributes one high EQ to complete the table row, as shown here.

External Inquiries	$2 \times 3 = 6$	$1 \times 6 = 6$	12

The final function point count is 108, as shown in Table 11.8. This count must next be adjusted based on the 14 IFPUG General System Characteristics (GSCs).

11.3 General System Characteristics

Once the unadjusted function points have been calculated, 14 (IFPUG) General System Characteristics (GSCs) must be considered and factored into the final function point total. Each factor is given an adjustment weight of 0 to 5, as shown in Table 11.9 [Jones, 1998]. The GSCs are listed in Table 11.10 below, and the table will be completed when each of the factors has been considered.

Table 11.8.   Cyber Order System Unadjusted Function Points

Type of Component	Complexity Low	Complexity Average	Complexity High	Total
External Inputs		$1 \times 4 = 4$	$2 \times 6 = 12$	16
External Outputs	$5 \times 4 = 20$	$3 \times 5 = 15$		35
External Inquiries	$2 \times 3 = 6$		$1 \times 6 = 6$	12
Internal Logical Files	$5 \times 7 = 35$			35
External Interface Files	$2 \times 5 = 10$			10
			Total Unadjusted Function Point Count (UFPC)	108

11.3.1 Data Communications

This application must support ordering over the Internet as well as remote printing of a pick list at warehouse locations. From the GSC Data Communications table (see Appendix C), an adjustment weight of 3 is assigned.

Adjustment factor $= 3$

11.3.2 Distributed Functions

How are distributed data and processing functions handled? The event-response distribution matrix and the data entity distribution matrix are presented in

Table 11.9.   Component Complexity Weights

0	Not present or no influence at all
1	Minor influence
2	Moderate influence
3	Average influence
4	Significant influence
5	Strong, pervasive influence

Table 11.10.   General System Characteristics

Data communications	Online update
Distributed functions	Complex processing
Performance goals	Reusability
Configuration usage	Installation ease
Transaction rates	Operational ease
Onine data entry	Multiple-site usage
End-user efficiency	Facilitate change

Tables 11.11 and 11.12, respectively. An examination of these models will aid in the determination of the rating of this factor. Processing and data are distributed to Chicago, Indianapolis, and Dallas, and data is transferred among all three locations.

Adjustment factor = 4

Table 11.11.   Event-Response Distribution Matrix

Event Response	Chicago Distribution	Indy Order Entry	Indy Customer Service	Indy Inventory Control	Indy Purchasing	Dallas Customer Service
Fill order		√				
Return item			√			√
Add customer		√	√			√
Record discount information		√				
Produce item availability	√	√	√	√	√	√
Generate daily sales report			√	√	√	√

Table 11.12.   Data Entity Distribution Matrix

Data Entity	Chicago Distri-bution	Indy Order Entry	Indy Customer Service	Indy Inventory Control	Indy Purchasing	Dallas Customer Service
Customer	R	CR	CR	R	R	CR
Item Discount		CU				
Item	R	RU	RU	R	R	RU
Order		C	R	R	R	R
Ordered Item		C	R	R	R	R

C = Create, R = Read, U = Update

11.3.3 Performance Goals

Examine the event-response specifications for this information. For this example, response time for *Fill Order* is critical during all business hours and requires performance analysis in the design phase.

Adjustment factor = 4

11.3.4 Configuration Usage

This operational configuration will be scaled to meet the required response time.

Adjustment factor = 0

11.3.5 Transaction Rates

This information should have been captured during the joint sessions and documented in the event-response specifications. Transaction rates are expected to be as high as 300 per hour, and performance is a critical issue during design.

Adjustment factor = 4

11.3.6 Online Data Entry

This is a physical design issue, but the analysis team often has a fairly good idea following requirements definition. What percentage of the information is entered online? For this application, most transactions will be entered interactively.

Adjustment factor = 5

11.3.7 End-user Efficiency

The design of online functions include the following components, but no specific requirements were given.

Navigational aids
Menus
Online help
Remote printing
Use of function keys
A mouse interface
Pop-up windows
Minimal screens

Adjustment factor = 3

11.3.8 Online Update

How many ILFs are updated by an online transaction? Using the CRUD matrix, the following file types are updated and automatic back-up and restore is required.

3 fundamental
1 attributive (weak)
1 associative

Adjustment factor = 5

11.3.9 Complex Processing

Examine the event-response specifications to determine processing complexity. This application requires audit processing, but most other processing is straightforward.

Adjustment factor = 1

11.3.10 Reusability

The components of this application will not be designed for use in other systems.

Adjustment factor = 0

11.3.11 Installation Ease

No special installation considerations are required.

Adjustment factor = 0

11.3.12 Operational Ease

This application is designed for operator intervention in the start-up, back-up, and recovery procedures; tape mounts are minimal.

Adjustment factor = 2

11.3.13 Multiple-site Usage

This application was specifically designed, developed, and supported to be installed at multiple sites with similar environments. An examination of the geographic location list will be helpful when determining this factor.

Location list:

Chicago

distribution (4 workstations)

Indianapolis

order entry (5 workstations)

customer service (3 workstations)

inventory control (3 workstations)

purchasing (3 workstations)

Dallas

customer service (4 workstations)

Adjustment factor = 4

11.3.14 Facilitate Change

The application was specifically designed, developed, and supported to facilitate flexible query and report capabilities of average complexity applied to more than one file.

Adjustment factor = 2

11.4 Adjustment to Function Points

Finally, the degrees of influence determined in Section 11.3 and shown in Table 11.13 are summed to arrive at a total influence on function points (37). This sum is then adjusted on the basis of the following equation giving the Value Adjustment Factor (VAF).

$$VAF = 0.65 + (0.01 \times 37) = 1.02$$

Table 11.13.   GSC Adjustment Factors

Data communications	3	Online update	5
Distributed functions	4	Complex processing	1
Performance goals	4	Reusability	0
Configuration usage	0	Installation ease	0
Transaction rates	4	Operational ease	2
Online data entry	5	Multiple-site usage	4
End-user efficiency	3	Facilitate change	2

The VAF is applied to the Function Point Count (FPC) derived from the original five system components, as shown below.

$$FPC = UFPC \times VAF = 108 \times 1.02 = 110$$

The final FPC is a measure of the size of the proposed system based largely on the conceptual system requirements. Using the midpoint of the normal range for U.S. software projects of 7.5 function points per staff-month, 110 function points would take approximately 15 staff-months to complete.

11.5 Example Summary

Examination of the individual event responses from the requirements models gave us an initial count of 108 function points, representing the functionality of the proposed system. A more general evaluation of the project size that considers non-coding tasks returned an adjustment factor of 1.02 and affected the final FPC very little.

For a small project such as the one represented in this example, about 50 percent of the effort will be coding. For a much larger project, as little as 15 percent of the total effort is coding, and so a much higher adjustment factor would be expected.

PART IV

Object-Partitioned Response to Events

Regardless of the internal organization, the primary function of an information system, in its simplest form, is fundamentally the same. It accepts data as input and, based on business rules, transforms it into output. But the organization of the software that produces the output can vary significantly. There are many ways to define the components of a system.

The following chapters do not represent a methodology. They describe one perspective of an object-oriented approach to system *structure.* This view of objects can be foundational for understanding the methodologies that are available.

CHAPTER TWELVE

Common Techniques

- 12.1 Event-Driven User Interface
- 12.2 The System Response
- 12.3 Transitional Methods

12.1 Event-Driven User Interface

Most of the popular object-oriented methodologies of the 1990s recommend "use cases" to define the user interface with the proposed system.

> **Use case.** A behaviorally related sequence of steps (a scenario), both automated and manual, for the purpose of completing a single business task [Whitten and Bentley, 1998].
>
> **Use case modeling.** The process of identifying and modeling business events, who initiated them, and how the system responds to them [Whitten and Bentley, 1998].

Use cases define business events; when taken to an elementary level, a single use case defines a single event. This commonality with an event interface makes much of the early modeling of Part II reusable when following an object-oriented strategy. The behavioral model, the data model, and the event diagrams of the processing model are all relevant to the requirements effort when objects will be used. It is not necessary to "start over" when documenting requirements for an object-oriented environment.

12.2 The System Response

In Part II, the internal organization method is based on events. All the processing needed to respond to one business event—that is, the user interface, business-rule processing, and database interface—is contained in one conceptual partition of the system.

But with an object-oriented approach and an object class as a partition, the conceptual response to a business event is not contained in a single system partition. Instead, it is spread as services (methods) among multiple partitions (object classes) that must then collaborate to respond to the business event. A single event response must be decomposed before it can be dispersed across the object classes. Object-oriented partitioning takes place at a level below that of event partitioning.

Event partition: that part of an information system that responds to a single business event.

Object partition: that part of an information system that contains the data and processing for a single object class.

12.3 Transitional Methods

Many object-oriented methodologies are available, and the more popular ones are elegant and thorough and quite different from each other. The creators of these methods seem to have had uniqueness as one of their major objectives. Generally, these methodologies don't build on an existing approach and, consequently, don't make use of an existing knowledge base.

Gerald Weinberg, in his book *An Introduction to General Systems Thinking* [1975], expresses an idea he calls "The Lump Law": "If we want to learn anything, we mustn't try to learn everything." This idea, as it might apply to learning a new methodology, would be to begin with a methodology that is close to or a derivation of one that is already known and has been used before. This is a smaller step to take than adopting a methodology that is new in most all aspects. After gaining experience with a transitional methodology, one can take another, smaller step and move to a methodology that was developed new from the ground up. To abandon years of experience by following a totally new set of techniques increases the learning curve and reduces productivity to an extent that many corporations are unwilling to accept.

Most organizations cannot afford to shut down development for months while their information systems development group switches to a totally new approach. When changing paradigms, it makes sense to seek a transitional set of techniques to reuse experience and reduce the cost of switchover. The foundation of this transitional methodology is that, even though an object-oriented methodology is partitioned around objects, the system must still respond to the events occurring in the business. There is no apparent reason to document a business event and the system response differently from one methodology to another.

The purpose of "Object-Partitioned Response to Events" is to provide an understanding of the fundamental elements of an object-oriented approach and to present the commonality and the differences between event partitioning and object partitioning. It presents some techniques for object-partitioned requirements analysis and specification based on an event-driven user interface (as used in Part II). An attempt has been made to use as many of the methods from the event-partitioned approach as possible as long as they contribute value to the overall process. This continuity of approach reuses current knowledge and allows for a more efficient transition from the modern event-driven methods to one based on object classes.

12.3.1 Behavior Model

System behavior focuses on activities outside the system boundary and a high-level specification of the system response. The users of the system, the business events that drive the system, the inputs that will trigger a response from the system, and the outputs produced by the system all describe the system behavior. The main difference in an object-oriented approach is that objects will collaborate to generate a response to a business event.

Five artifacts make up the system behavior documentation and are described in detail in Chapter 5. No further explanation is necessary in this chapter.

- Business Event List

- System Response Table

- System Context Diagram

- Business Event Scenarios

- Functional Decomposition Diagram

12.3.2 Data Model

Another model that is reusable from the event-partitioned approach is the data model. Stored data must contain those classes and data attributes that a business area will need to store to support their information systems. The data model will

- Identify real-world business entities about which data is stored

- Document relevant relationships between the data entities

- Define data attributes

- Be normalized into a stable, effective configuration of entities

The Entity Relationship Diagram (ERD) described in Chapter 6 will work well for an object-oriented approach. The components of the modeling effort are

- Object classes

- Class hierarchy

- Class associations

- Class attributes

- Data normalization

12.3.3 Process Model

The Behavior Model defines, at a high level, the system response to each business event. But to this point, the detailed processing has not been considered.

The process model uses Data Flow Diagrams (DFDs) to document the required input and output, along with the data transformation rules for each event response. When an object-oriented approach is followed, each event response will be disassembled and reassembled into an object-partitioned structure. Development and specification of event diagrams will be virtually the same in both approaches. The Event Diagram and the decomposition of the event response require no change from Chapter 7. From this point on, however, the response to a business event must be structured very differently if it is going to dovetail with the object environment used for design and construction. It can no longer be contained in a single processing unit. The system response to an event must now involve multiple object classes in a collaboration effort. This requires a different modeling technique.

12.3.4 Object Partitioning

The "Function Assembly by Class" and "CRUD Associations" describe the distribution of event-response components to the appropriate object class. It must then be determined how the classes can interface to produce the required response for the system's users. Chapter 14, Class Interaction, maps the functions back to a single event response and defines messages designed to facilitate the collaboration of the classes. It also examines the isolation of application-specific functionality to an *application control class* to hold the processing that is unique to each event response and does not fit into one of the general-purpose classes. Finally, a diagram of the interaction of objects will provide a map for system development in subsequent phases. The Object Class Interaction Diagram identifies the classes involved with each event response and documents the necessary message paths.

CHAPTER THIRTEEN

Class Operations

- **13.1 Function Assembly by Class**
- **13.2 CRUD Associations**

The models developed thus far (event list and system response table) do not provide sufficient detail from which to develop or generate system programs. Event responses have been represented as "black boxes," and system inputs and outputs have been named but not defined to the attribute level.

The process model further specifies the system components with Data Flow Diagrams (DFDs). For an object-oriented approach, the event models will be developed as in an event-partitioned approach but will then be disassembled and reassembled into a class-based structure. The event diagrams and related specifications will provide input to this effort.

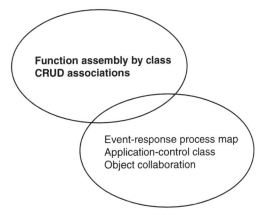

Function assembly by class
CRUD associations

Event-response process map
Application-control class
Object collaboration

13.1 Function Assembly by Class

To this point in the requirements definition, a response to a business event has been organized into a single processing unit. In an object-partitioned approach, this must change. Even though the system will respond to individual business events, it will now become a collaboration effort between object classes.

Assembly of function by class reorganizes the event-response process fragments by moving them to the appropriate class as methods and data. The class is based on the database entities and the user/device interfaces required by the event response.

Assembly of function reuses, for the development of class data and processing (methods), the event-response diagram and specification previously completed. It begins the effort to partition the system processing around object classes rather than the events found in the business.

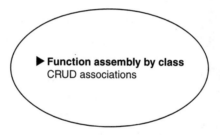

▶ **Function assembly by class**
CRUD associations

13.1.1 Technique

Refer to the Event Diagram for Fill Order (Section 7.1.2) for the partial example that follows.

- Establish a class for each data entity in the Event Diagram; in many cases, some of these classes will already exist.

  Customer
  Order
  Ordered Item
  Item
  Item Discount

- Using the definition of each data entity from the data model, establish the attributes as properties of each class.

- Using the pseudocode from the Event Diagram (Section 7.3.2), add to each class the methods required to serve the *Fill Order* processing.

- Document the interface to each method using method name and a parameter list.

13.1.2 Example

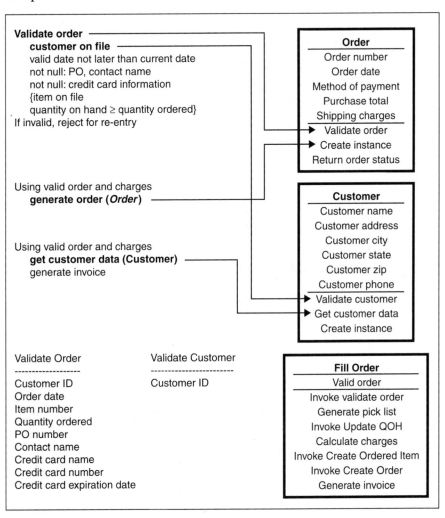

Figure 13.1   Assembly of function by class

13.1.3 Risk if Not Completed

To have an object-partitioned system, the functionality identified in the event responses must be dispersed among the object classes.

13.1.4 Technique Tips

- While the assembly effort can be accomplished using the pseudocode, the effort may be aided by the leveling of the Event Diagram. It is a question of balance between schedule and the time required for development of the leveled diagrams.

- The pseudocode can contain any information that is valuable to the assembly effort. For example, in Figure 13.1, the data store from which information is retrieved is shown in italics.

- Subsequent to the assembly effort, the collaboration of the classes required to respond to a business event will be documented. This will conceptually reunite the pieces of the event response that have been dispersed to the object classes.

- Each stored-data class will need methods to perform the custodial functions: create, read, update, and delete.

13.2 CRUD Associations

The acronym CRUD represents the custodial functions of a typical database entity—that is, Create, Retrieve, Update, and Delete. Each table or file in a database must have these functions from the system under design or from another system.

In an event-partitioned system, the CRUD matrix provides a means of examining the interaction between data entities in the data model and event responses from the System Response Table (SRT) by documenting which of the four functions each event response provides for each data entity. Any entity without all four CRUD functions will require further examination of the proposed system for missing functionality. In an object-partitioned system, the CRUD matrix shows which data classes collaborate for the completion of the event response and which data functions each class contributes. Application-control and user-interface classes contribute little value to the matrix.

The CRUD matrix provides a means of examining the interaction between object classes and event responses and validates the completeness of the proposed system design. It also documents data dependencies between event responses for use in designing multiple releases of a system.

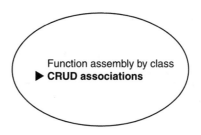

13.2.1 Technique

- Build a matrix with the data entities on one axis and the event responses on the other.

- At each intersection of a row and column (each cell), record which of the four CRUD functions the event response provides for that data entity (from zero to all four).

- Examine each row or column, whichever has the data entities, for all four CRUD functions. If any function is missing for an entity, it must be determined whether it is the responsibility of the system under development or of another system.

- Note from the example that instances of Item are not created in the system as defined here. Item was not shown to be outside of the system in the context diagram (where another system would create these instances), so there is no apparent explanation for the fact that Item instances are not created.

13.2.2 Example

Table 13.1.   Cyber Order System CRUD Matrix

Event Response	Customer	Item Discount	Item	Order	Ordered Item
Fill order	R	R	RU	C	C
Process return	R		RU	R	R
Add customer	C				
Record discount information		CU	R		

(continued)

Table 13.1. *(continued)*

Event Response	Customer	Item Discount	Item	Order	Ordered Item
Produce item availability	R		R		
Generate daily sales report	R			R	R

C = Create, R = Read, U = Update

13.2.3 Risk if Not Completed

Required processes that are not evident from the business event analysis might be missed. Also, a means of examining how data classes collaborate for the completion of the event response would not be available.

13.2.4 Technique Tips

- Use the CRUD matrix to map the interaction between classes for the completion of an event response

- Some methodologies suggest listing only the most significant function in each cell. It is suggested here that any and all of the functions that are provided by the event response be shown.

- Use the event diagrams when building the CRUD matrix, since they show all interfaces with the data entities.

- Refer to the process specs when building the CRUD matrix, because they offer detail information about interfaces with the data entities.

- The CRUD matrix shows data dependencies. For example, when an event response is reading a data entity, it can be determined which other event response (or responses) creates or updates that entity. The functionality requiring the read cannot be implemented without the create and update functions.

CHAPTER FOURTEEN

Class Interaction

- **14.1 Event-Response Process Map**
- **14.2 Application-Control Class**
- **14.3 Object Collaboration**

In an object-partitioned system, the required functions of each event response are dispersed among the object classes. The object classes must collaborate to produce a response to a request from the environment in which the system resides. During the specification of class operations, the total response to a business event was documented. It must now be determined how the classes can interface to produce that required response for the system's users.

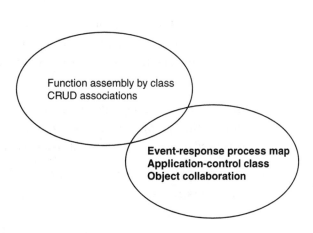

Function assembly by class
CRUD associations

Event-response process map
Application-control class
Object collaboration

14.1 Event-Response Process Map

The required response components of each event are spread across multiple object classes. These functions must be mapped back to a single event response, and messages must be designed to facilitate the collaboration of the classes designed. The sequencing of event-response functionality provides a basis for this mapping.

The event diagrams and the pseudocode hold the information needed to design a configuration of object messages that will generate a response to a business event. The deliverable is a documentation of the functions of each event response and their process sequence.

This section prepares the pseudocode for use in the development of the object collaboration map.

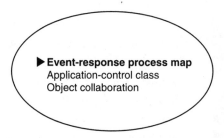

▶ **Event-response process map**
Application-control class
Object collaboration

14.1.1 Technique

- The input to this effort is made up of the event diagram, the pseudocode, and the data flow specifications (see Chapter 7).

- Document the sequence of the processing components reflected in the pseudocode (refer to (1) *Validate Order* and (2) *Next Order Number* in Figure 14.1). When functions can be executed in parallel, identify them with the same number.

- Using the event diagram along with the sequenced processes, associate the name of the appropriate method from the Class Operation effort with the sequenced processing component, as shown in the example.

- The deliverable is the pseudocode for an event response marked up as shown in Figure 14.1.

14.1.2 Example

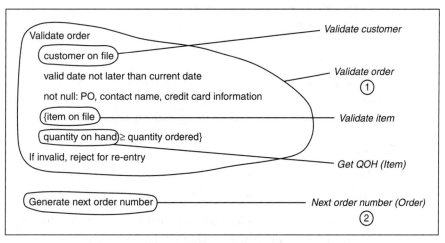

Figure 14.1   *Fill Order* event-response process map

For each valid item
    Using valid order
        get item information (Item)
        add to pick list
    Using valid order
        get QOH (Item)
        update QOH
    Using valid order
        get item price (Item)
        get price discount percentage for order date (Item Discount)
        calculate charges ((Item price * quantity ordered) * tax rate)
    Using valid order and charges
        generate order item (Ordered Item)
End For

Using order number
    generate pick list
Using valid order and charges
    generate order (Order)

Using valid order and charges
get customer information (Customer)
generate invoice

14.1.3 Risk if Not Completed

For this approach, the pseudocode must be examined to direct the object collaboration definition effort and is required for the design of the application-control class. How it is documented is largely up to the developer.

14.1.4 Technique Tips

- This effort must include all pseudocode to account for the entire processing requirements of an event response.

- The methods in the application class (developed as part of the object collaboration effort) will act as a guide to validate this effort.

- The name of the method is included in italics.

- The name of the class can be included following the method name when it adds necessary value to the diagram.

14.2 Application-Control Class

One of the key properties of an object-oriented approach is the opportunity and the mindset to reuse both data and processing. Isolation of application-specific functionality to an application control class keeps the common-use classes highly cohesive and preserves and maximizes the opportunity for reuse.

An application class holds the processing that is unique to each event response and provides an interface to remote classes such as a menu class. A large part of the responsibility of an application class is to control the sequence of the interfaces with static domain classes such as a stored-data class.

Development of an application class captures the sequence of processing and documents the processing that does not naturally fit into other classes. It isolates application-specific functionality.

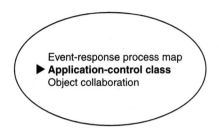

14.2.1 Technique

- Using the sequenced pseudocode from *Event-Response Process Map,* establish an application class with methods to control the event-response processing. From the example: (1) *Validate Order* and (2) *Next Order Number.*

- Implement methods for required business rules that are not associated with a specific stored-data class.

14.2.2 Example

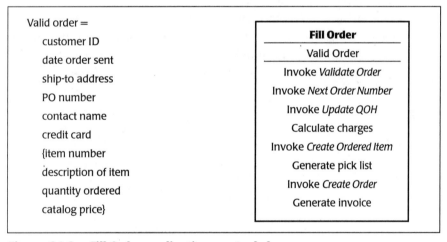

Figure 14.2 *Fill Order* **application-control class**

14.2.3 Risk if Not Completed

This is a philosophical issue. Placing application- (event-response-) specific processing in static object classes that are fundamental to the business creates lower cohesion. This also disperses the application processing, making it more difficult to respond when the business changes.

14.2.4 Technique Tips

- The application class can take on the interface responsibilities such as interfacing with a menu class.

- The application class typically should receive the trigger from the event response.

14.3 Object Collaboration

The necessary processing for each event response is distributed across object classes. A diagram of the interaction of objects will provide a map for system development in subsequent phases.

The object class interaction diagram identifies the classes involved with the event response and documents the necessary message paths. It is similar in nature to a Data Flow Diagram (DFD) in that the rectangle represents processing while the arrows represent data in the form of messages and arguments passing between the processing units.

This section fills the gap between the object-partitioned system functions and the obligation of the system to respond to individual business events. It maps out a reunion of the functions of a single system response; it abstractly reassembles each event response from the collaborating object classes.

Event-response process map
Application-control class
▶ **Object collaboration**

14.3.1 Technique

For each event response:

- Begin the diagram with an application class.

- Using the first processing unit in the sequence established in the preceding section along with the application class, identify the object class and method that must be invoked first; add them to the diagram.

- Connect the object class to the application class with a message line.

- Continue adding classes and methods to the diagram following the sequence of processing components in the pseudocode and connect them with the appropriate message path.

- Optionally, place the sequence number on each message (see Figure 14.1).

- Title and label the diagram as shown in Figure 14.3.

14.3.2 Example

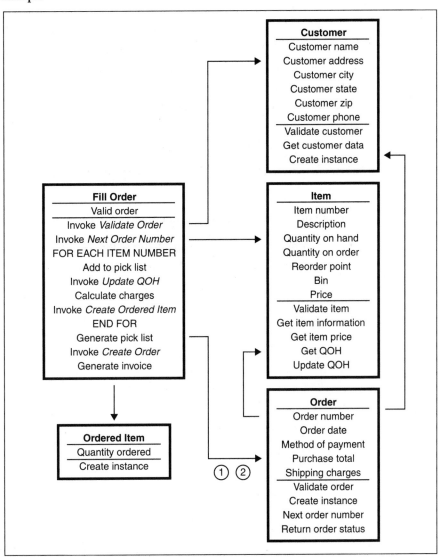

Figure 14.3 *Fill Order* **object-collaboration map**

14.3.3 Risk if Not Completed

Subsequent phases will need to know the methods involved with an event response and the object classes responsible for invoking them. Risk is associated with delaying this specification to later phases.

14.3.4 Technique Tips

- Messages need not be defined since the interface to each method has already been specified.

- "A Message Connection combines event-response and data flow perspectives, that is, each Message Connection represents a message being sent, as well as a response being received. Message Connections are used to accommodate Service needs

  "A Message Connection maps one instance with another, in which a 'sender' sends a message to a 'receiver,' to get some processing done" [Coad and Yourdon, 1990].

- The arrow points from the class that initiates the message to the receiving class.

- Data contained in each message is documented in the method specification.

- Some may object to the placement of the sequence numbers on the messages. It certainly is not critical, but it adds information to the diagram.

Collection of Examples

Event List

Some of the events listed below are not supported by the abbreviated data model.

1. Customer places order
2. Customer returns item
3. Person requests customer status
4. Management submits item discount information
5. Customer inquires about item availability
6. Time to generate daily sales report

Business Event Scenario

An order clerk receives an order from the customer and must collect the required information. The data making up the order is entered into and validated by the computer system. The clerk must be notified of any invalid data and have the option of correcting that data immediately. The system must also check the on-hand quantity of any item ordered and advise the clerk if the amount ordered is not available. An option to partial fill and back order is required when an insufficient quantity exists. When an order is completed, the system should have produced the following.

- Updated inventory counts

- A customer invoice

- A pick list for the warehouse

- A packing slip for the warehouse

System Response Table

Table 5.1.   Cyber Order System—System Response Table

Event	Source	Trigger	Event Response	Major Output	External Destination
E1	Customer	Order	Fill order	• Invoice • Order • Inventory update • Pick list	• Customer • Warehouse • Database
E2	Customer	Item	Process return	• Inventory update • Damaged item list	• Database • Management
E3	Candidate customer	Customer status request	Add customer	• New customer	• Database
E4	Management	Discount information	Record discount information	• Validated discount information	• Database
E5	Customer	Item availability request	Produce item availability	• Item availability	• Customer
E6		(Temporal)	Generate daily sales report	• Daily sales report	• Sales department

A variation of this table may be preferable for some development teams. For example, some teams omit the last two columns.

Context Diagram

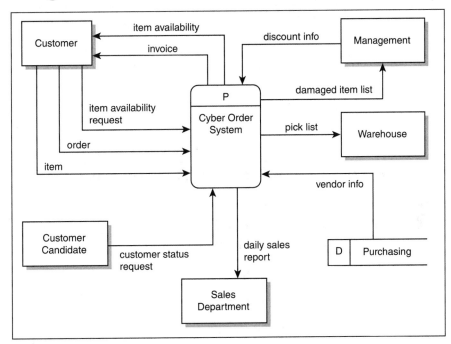

Figure 5.1   Cyber Order System Context Diagram

Functional Decomposition

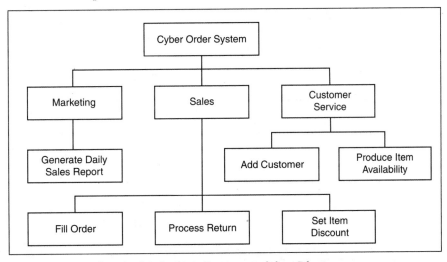

Figure 5.2   Cyber Order System Decomposition Diagram

Fundamental Entities

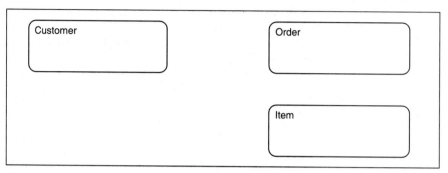

Figure 6.1   Cyber Order System fundamental entities

Other entities that will be identified as the data model evolves as relationships and attributes are added include the following.

- Commercial Order (subtype)

- Individual Order (subtype)

- Item Discount (attributive)

- Item Return (attributive)

- Ordered Item (associative)

Entity Relationships

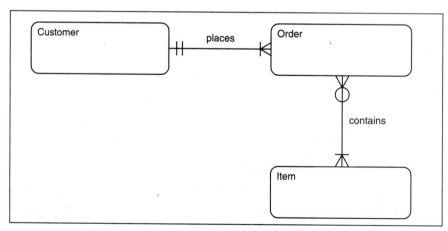

Figure 6.2   Cyber Order System relationships

- One customer can place many orders.

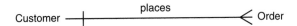

- A particular order can be placed by only one customer.

- One customer must have placed at least one order.

- An order must have been placed by at least one customer.

- Other relationship examples:

    "item is assigned an item discount"

    "an order contains order items"

    "an item is contained on an order item"

Entity Attributes

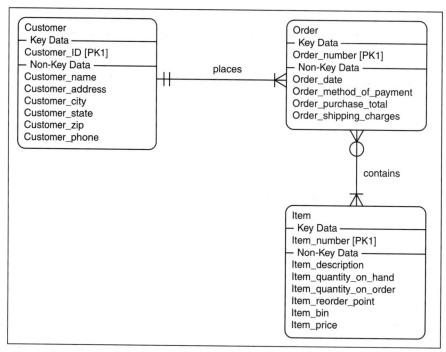

Figure 6.3   Cyber Order System entity attributes

properties of *Customer name*:

    data type: character

    length: 30

    domain: any alphabetic character and a dash (-)

    null validity: null not allowed

Normalization

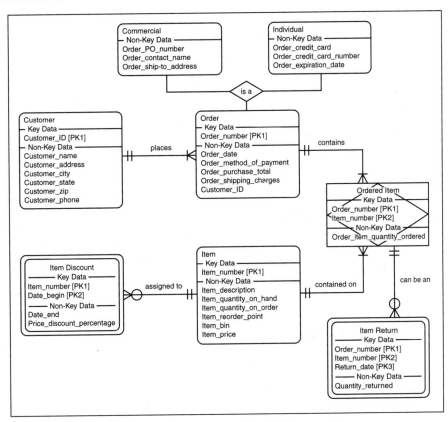

Figure 6.4   Cyber Order System normalized data model

Event Diagram

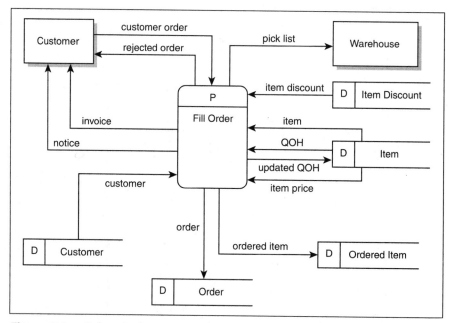

Figure 7.1   Cyber Order System Event Diagram

Leveled Event Diagram

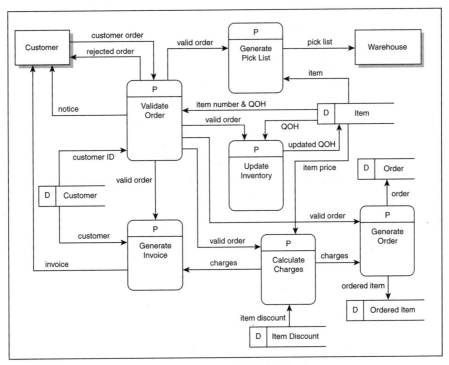

Figure 7.2   Cyber Order System Leveled Event Diagram

Process Specification

Validate order

customer on file

valid date not later than current date

not null: PO, contact name, credit card information

{item on file

numeric quantity }

If invalid, reject for re-entry

Generate next order number

For each valid item

Using valid order

If quantity on hand less than quantity ordered

```
                    generate notice
                End If
            Using valid order
                get item information (Item)
                add to pick list
            Using valid order
                get QOH (Item)
                update QOH
            Using valid order
                get item price (Item)
                get price discount percentage for order date (Item Discount)
                calculate charges (BR 1)
            Using valid order and charges
                generate ordered item (Ordered Item)
        End For

        Using order number
            generate pick list
        Using valid order and charges
            generate order (Order)
        Using valid order and charges
            get customer information (Customer)
            generate invoice
```

BR 1: ((((Item price * Item price discount) * quantity ordered) * tax rate)

Customer order =	Ship-to address =	Pick list =
customer ID	recipient name	order number
date order sent	street address	{item number
ship-to address	city	item description
PO number	state	item bin
contact name	zip	quantity ordered}
credit card		
{item number	Credit card =	
description of item	credit card name	
quantity ordered	credit card number	
catalog price }	credit card expiration date	

Notice =
> order number
> customer ID
> customer phone
> date order sent
> item number
> item description
> order item quantity ordered

Invoice =
> customer ID
> customer name
> ship-to address
> {item number
> item description
> .order item quantity ordered
> item price}

CRUD Matrix

Table 8.1. Cyber Order System CRUD Matrix

Event Response	Customer	Item Discount	Item	Order	Ordered Item
Fill order	R	R	RU	C	C
Process return	R		RU	R	R
Add customer	C				
Record discount information		CU	R		
Produce item availability	R		R		
Generate daily sales report	R			R	R

C = Create, R = Read, U = Update

Entity Process View

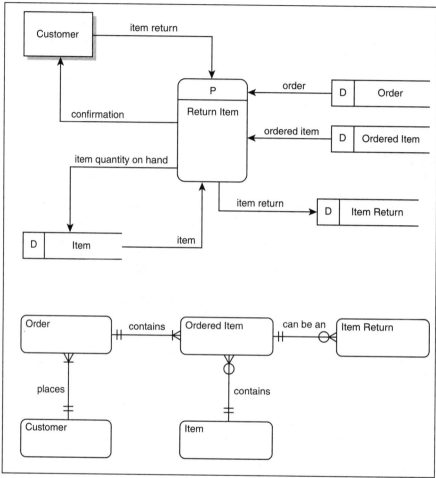

Figure 8.1   Cyber Order System Entity Process View

Entity Life Cycle Diagram

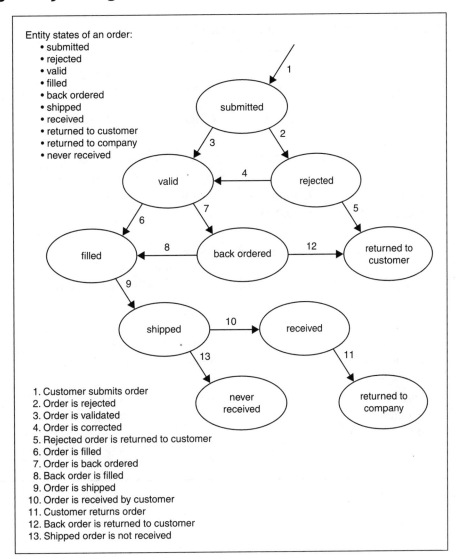

Entity states of an order:
- submitted
- rejected
- valid
- filled
- back ordered
- shipped
- received
- returned to customer
- returned to company
- never received

1. Customer submits order
2. Order is rejected
3. Order is validated
4. Order is corrected
5. Rejected order is returned to customer
6. Order is filled
7. Order is back ordered
8. Back order is filled
9. Order is shipped
10. Order is received by customer
11. Customer returns order
12. Back order is returned to customer
13. Shipped order is not received

Figure 8.2   Cyber Order System Entity Life Cycle Diagram

Release Identification

Table 9.1.   Cyber Order System–System Release Table

Business Event	Source	Trigger	Event Response	System Release
Customer places order	Customer	Order	Fill Order	1
Customer returns item	Customer	Item	Process return	1
Person requests customer status	Candidate customer	Customer status request	Add customer	1
Management submits item discount information	Management	Discount information	Record discount information	1
Customer inquires about item availability	Customer	Item availability request	Produce item availability	1
Time to generate daily sales report		(temporal)	Generate daily sales report	1

System Distribution

Location list:

    Chicago

        distribution (4)

    Indianapolis

        order entry (5)

        customer service (3)

        inventory control (3)

        purchasing (3)

    Dallas

        customer service (4)

Event-Response Distribution Matrix

Table 9.2.   Cyber Order System Event-Response Distribution Matrix

Event Response	Chicago Distribution	Indy Order Entry	Indy Customer Service	Indy Inventory Control	Indy Purchasing	Dallas Customer Service
Fill order		√				
Process return			√			√
Add customer		√	√			√
Record discount information		√				
Produce item availability	√	√	√	√	√	√
Generate daily sales report			√	√	√	√

Data Entity Distribution Matrix

Table 9.3.　Cyber Order System Data Entity Distribution Matrix

Data Entity	Chicago Distribution	Indy Order Entry	Indy Customer Service	Indy Inventory Control	Indy Purchasing	Dallas Customer Service
Customer	R	CR	CR	R	R	CR
Item discount		CU				
Item	R	RU	RU	R	R	RU
Order		C	R	R	R	R
Ordered item		C	R	R	R	R

C = Create, R = Read, U = Update

Model Notation and Symbols

Entity Relationship Diagram

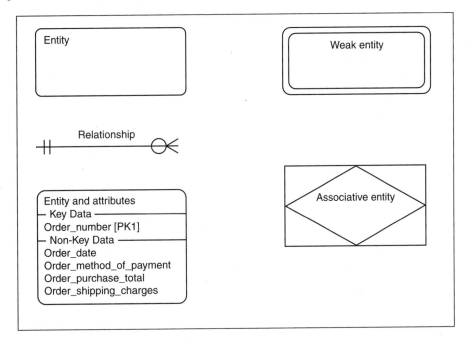

Data Flow Diagram

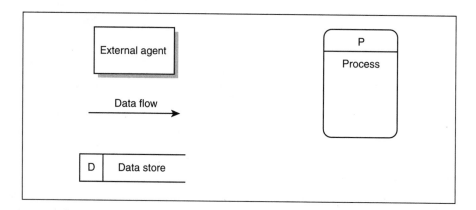

Entity Life Cycle

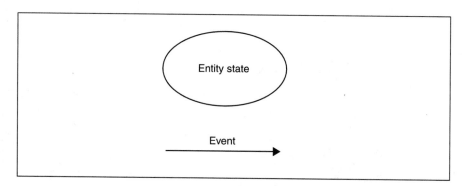

Object Classes

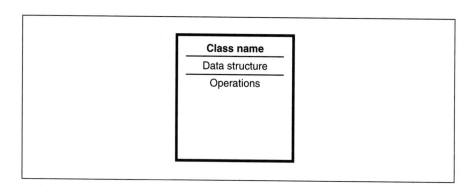

IFPUG* General System Characteristics Tables

Data Communications

The *data* and *control* information used in the application are sent or received over communications facilities. Terminals connected locally to the control unit are considered to use communications facilities. Protocol is a set of conventions that permit the transfer or exchange of information between two systems or devices. All data communication links require some type of protocol.

Table C.1.   Data Communications Degree of Influence

Score as	Descriptions to Determine Degree of Influence
0	Application is pure batch processing or a standalone PC.
1	Application is batch but has remote data entry *or* remote printing.
2	Application is batch but has remote data entry *and* remote printing.
3	Application includes online data collection or TP (teleprocessing) front end to a batch process or query system.
4	Application is more than a front end but supports only one type of TP communications protocol.
5	Application is more than a front end and supports more than one type of TP communications protocol.

*The International Function Point Users Group (IFPUG) is a not-for-profit, member-run user group. IFPUG's mission is to be a recognized leader in promoting and encouraging the effective management of application software development and maintenance activities through the use of Function Point Analysis and other software measurement techniques. For more information, go to *www.ifpug.org* or contact IFPUG—e-mail: *ifpug@ifpug.org,* phone: (614) 895-7130, fax: (614) 895-3466.

Distributed Data Processing

Distributed data or processing functions are characteristics of the application within the application boundary.

Table C.2.   **Distributed Data Processing Degree of Influence**

Score as	Descriptions to Determine Degree of Influence
0	Application does not aid the transfer of data or processing function between components of the system.
1	Application prepares data for end-user processing on another component of the system such as PC spreadsheets and PC DBMS.
2	Data is prepared for transfer, then is transferred and processed on another component of the system (not for end-user processing).
3	Distributed processing and data transfer are online and in one direction only.
4	Distributed processing and data transfer are online and in both directions.
5	Processing functions are dynamically performed on the most appropriate component of the system.

Performance

Application performance objectives, stated or approved by the user, *in either* response or throughput, influence (or will influence) the design, development, installation, and support of the application.

Table C.3.   Performance Degree of Influence

Score as	Descriptions to Determine Degree of Influence
0	No special performance requirements were stated by the user.
1	Performance and design requirements were stated and reviewed, but no special actions were required.
2	Response time or throughput is critical during peak hours. No special design for CPU utilization was required. Processing deadline is for the next business day.
3	Response time or throughput is critical during all business hours. No special design for CPU utilization was required. Processing deadline requirements with interfacing systems are constraining.
4	In addition, stated user performance requirements are stringent enough to require performance analysis tasks in the design phase.
5	In addition, performance analysis tools were used in the design, development, and/or implementation phases to meet the stated user performance requirements.

Heavily Used Configuration

A heavily used operational configuration, requiring special design considerations, is a characteristic of the application. For example, the user wants to run the application on existing or committed equipment that will be heavily used.

Table C.4.   Heavily Used Configuration Degree of Influence

Score as	Descriptions to Determine Degree of Influence
0	No explicit or implicit operational restrictions are included.
1	Operational restrictions exist, but they are less restrictive than a typical application. No special effort is needed to meet the restrictions.
2	Some security or timing considerations are included.
3	Specific processor requirements for a specific piece of the application are included.
4	Stated operation restrictions require special constraints on the application in the central processor or a dedicated processor.
5	In addition, there are special constraints on the application in the distributed components of the system.

Transaction Rate

The transaction rate is high, and it influenced the design, development, installation, and support of the application.

Table C.5. Transaction Rate Degree of Influence

Score as	Descriptions to Determine Degree of Influence
0	No peak transaction period is anticipated.
1	Peak transaction period (e.g., monthly, quarterly, seasonally, annually) is anticipated.
2	Weekly peak transaction period is anticipated.
3	Daily peak transaction period is anticipated.
4	High transaction rate(s) stated by the user in the application requirements or service level agreements are high enough to require performance analysis tasks in the design phase.
5	High transaction rate(s) stated by the user in the application requirements or service level agreements are high enough to require performance analysis tasks and, in addition, require the use of performance analysis tools in the design, development, and/or installation phases.

Online Data Entry

Online data entry and control functions are provided in the application.

Table C.6.   Online Data Entry Degree of Influence

Score as	Descriptions to Determine Degree of Influence
0	All transactions are processed in batch mode.
1	1% to 7% of transactions are interactive data entry.
2	8% to 15% of transactions are interactive data entry.
3	16% to 23% of transactions are interactive data entry.
4	24% to 30% of transactions are interactive data entry.
5	More than 30% of transactions are interactive data entry.

End-User Efficiency

The online functions provided emphasize a design for end-user efficiency. The design includes

- Navigational aids (for example, function keys, jumps, dynamically generated menus)

- Menus

- Online help and documents

- Automated cursor movement

- Scrolling

- Remote printing (via online transactions)

- Preassigned function keys

- Batch jobs submitted from online transactions

- Cursor selection of screen data

- Heavy use of reverse video, highlighting, color underlining, and other indicators

- Hard copy user documentation of online transactions

- Mouse interface

- Pop-up windows

- As few screens as possible to accomplish a business function

- Bilingual support (supports two languages; count as four items)

- Multilingual support (supports more than two languages; count as six items)

Table C.7.   End-User Efficiency Degree of Influence

Score as	Descriptions to Determine Degree of Influence
0	None of the above.
1	One to three of the above.
2	Four to five of the above.
3	Six or more of the above, but there are no specific user requirements related to efficiency.
4	Six or more of the above, and stated requirements for end-user efficiency are strong enough to require design tasks for human factors to be included (for example, minimize key strokes, maximize defaults, use of templates).
5	Six or more of the above, and stated requirements for end-user efficiency are strong enough to require use of special tools and processes to demonstrate that the objectives have been achieved.

Online Update

The application provides online update for the Internal Logical Files (ILFs).

Table C.8.   Online Update Degree of Influence

Score as	Descriptions to Determine Degree of Influence
0	None.
1	Online update of one to three control files is included. Volume of updating is low and recovery is easy.
2	Online update of four or more control files is included. Volume of updating is low and recovery is easy.
3	Online update of major ILFs is included.
4	In addition, protection against data loss is essential and has been specially designed and programmed into the system.
5	In addition, high volumes bring cost considerations into the recovery process. Highly automated recovery procedures with minimum operator intervention are included.

Complex Processing

Complex processing is a characteristic of the application. The following components are present.

- Sensitive control (for example, special audit processing) and/or application-specific security processing

- Extensive logical processing

- Extensive mathematical processing

- Much exception processing resulting in incomplete transactions that must be processed again—for example, incomplete ATM transactions caused by TP interruption, missing data values, or failed edits

- Complex processing to handle multiple input/output possibilities—for example, multimedia, or device independence

Table C.9.   Complex Processing Degree of Influence

Score as	Descriptions to Determine Degree of Influence
0	None of the above
1	Any one of the above
2	Any two of the above
3	Any three of the above
4	Any four of the above
5	All five of the above

Reusability

The application and the code in the application have been specifically designed, developed, and supported to be usable in *other* applications.

Table C.10.   Reusability Degree of Influence

Score as	Descriptions to Determine Degree of Influence
0	No reusable code.
1	Reusable code is used within the application.
2	Less than 10 percent of the application considered more than one user's needs.
3	10 percent or more of the application considered more than one user's needs.
4	The application was specifically packaged and/or documented to ease reuse, and the application is customized by the user at source code level.
5	The application was specifically packaged and/or documented to ease reuse, and the application is customized for use by means of user parameter maintenance.

Installation Ease

Conversion and installation ease are characteristics of the application. A conversion and installation plan and/or conversion tools were provided and tested during the system test phase.

Table C.11.   Installation Ease Degree of Influence

Score as	Descriptions to Determine Degree of Influence
0	No special considerations were stated by the user, and no special set-up is required for installation.
1	No special considerations were stated by the user, *but* special set-up is required for installation.
2	Conversion and installation requirements were stated by the user, and conversion and installation guides were provided and tested. The impact of conversion on the project is not considered to be important.
3	Conversion and installation requirements were stated by the user, and conversion and installation guides were provided and tested. The impact of conversion on the project is considered to be important.
4	In addition to item 2 above, automated conversion and installation tools were provided and tested.
5	In addition to item 3 above, automated conversion and installation tools were provided and tested.

Operational Ease

Operational ease is characteristic of the application. Effective start-up, back-up, and recovery procedures were provided and tested during the system test phase. The application minimizes the need for manual activities, such as tape mounts, paper handling, and direct on-location manual intervention.

Table C.12.   Operational Ease Degree of Influence

Score as	Descriptions to Determine Degree of Influence
0	No special operational considerations other than the normal back-up procedures were stated by the user.
1–4	One, some, or all of the following items apply to the application. Select all that apply. Each item has a point value of 1, except as noted otherwise.
	Effective start-up, back-up, and recovery processes were provided, but operator intervention is required.
	Effective start-up, back-up, and recovery processes were provided, but no operator intervention is required (count as two items).
	The application minimizes the need for tape mounts.
	The application minimizes the need for paper handling.
5	The application is designed for unattended operation. Unattended operation means *no operator intervention* is required to operate the system other than to start up or shut down the application. Automatic error recovery is a feature of the application.

Multiple Sites

The application has been specifically designed, developed, and supported to be installed at multiple sites for multiple organizations.

Table C.13.   Multiple Sites Degree of Influence

Score as	Descriptions to Determine Degree of Influence
0	User requirements do not require consideration of the needs of more than one user/installation site.
1	Needs of multiple sites were considered in the design, and the application is designed to operate only *under identical* hardware and software environments.
2	Needs of multiple sites were considered in the design, and the application is designed to operate only *under similar* hardware and/or software environments.
3	Needs of multiple sites were considered in the design, and the application is designed to operate *under different* hardware and/or software environments.
4	Documentation and support plan are provided and tested to support the application at multiple sites and the application is as described in item 1 or 2.
5	Documentation and support plan are provided and tested to support the application at multiple sites and the application is as described in item 3.

Facilitate Change

The application has been specifically designed, developed, and supported to facilitate change. The following characteristics can apply for the application.

- Flexible query and report facility is provided that can handle simple requests—for example, *and/or* logic applied to only one ILF (count as one item).

- Flexible query and report facility is provided that can handle requests of average complexity—for example, *and/or* logic applied to more than one ILF (count as two items).

- Flexible query and report facility is provided that can handle complex requests—for example, *and/or* logic combinations on one or more ILFs (count as three items).

- Business control data is kept in tables that are maintained by the user with online interactive processes, but changes take effect only on the next business day.

- Business control data is kept in tables that are maintained by the user with online interactive processes, and the changes take effect immediately (count as two items).

Table C.14.   Facilitate Change Degree of Influence

Score as	Descriptions to Determine Degree of Influence
0	None of the above
1	Any one of the above
2	Any two of the above
3	Any three of the above
4	Any four of the above
5	All five of the above

Glossary

application: The set or a subset of the system's event responses designated to be delivered at the same time as a release or version of the system.

application control class: Holds the processing that is unique to each event response and does not fit into a data entity class; also provides an interface to remote classes such as a menu class.

associative entity: A data entity that stores information about a relationship and receives its identity (key) from the entities involved in the relationship. See **multiple occurrence associative key** and **single occurrence associative key**.

attribute: A data item that cannot be decomposed further. A property of an entity or class that holds a value for each occurrence of the entity or class.

attributive entity: A data entity that holds attributes that describe another entity. These attributes may repeat or may be null for a single instance of the original entity key. (Synonyms: *weak entity, dependent entity*)

black box: A unit of processing whose interfaces and function are known but whose internal logic is unknown.

BR (business rule): Used in the pseudo-code in this book to express the definition of a business rule in the processing of an event response.

business event: An activity in the user's environment that requires a response from the proposed information system.

cardinality: Defines the maximum and minimum number of instances in one entity that are linked to a single instance in another entity. Maximum cardinality can be 1 or more than 1. Minimum cardinality can be 0 (optional participation) or 1 (mandatory participation).

CASE (Computer Aided Software Engineering): Information technology tools that automate and support one or more phases of the system development life cycle.

client/server architecture: An architecture consisting of multiple systems or processes in which some of the functional roles (clients) request the services of other roles (servers) that service the requests. Servers provide services to requesting clients.

cohesion: The degree to which a system component accomplishes one and only one function.

concatenated key: A group of attributes (more than one) that uniquely identifies an instance of a data entity. A primary key composed of more than one data attribute.

conceptual: An abstract or generic idea generalized from particular instances [Webster's, 1994]. In IT, depicts *what* a system must do rather than *how* it will do it; nonphysical. (Synonym: *logical*)

core technique: A fundamental, non-proprietary technique that can apply to more than one commercial methodology.

coupling: The degree to which one system component is dependent on another.

Critical Success Factor (CSF): Something that must happen if an information system is to be successful.

CRUD matrix: A matrix that depicts the interaction between the data entities from the data model and the event responses by recording which of the custodial functions (create, read, update, and delete) are applied to the data by the processes.

custodial function: A function that is required for the creation, updating, and deletion of every data entity but is often not identified in the behavior model.

Data Element Type (DET): A data attribute, a column in a relational table, or a field in a record.

data flow: The representation of a packet of data that flows to or from a DFD process.

data flow definition: *See* **data flow specification**.

Data Flow Diagram (DFD): A graphic model that depicts the flow of data into and out of a system process and the transformation of the data that occurs.

data flow specification: A list and description of the attributes that will flow to or from a DFD process along a data flow.

data normalization: An activity that produces the proper configuration of entities along with the proper placement of attributes to reduce redundancy, eliminate data anomalies, and provide a data architecture that supports the effective and efficient retrieval and modification of data.

data store: A representation of data stored over time.

DBMS (Database Management System): A specialized software package that is used to manage the creation and maintenance of a database structure and that allows access to the data in the database.

deliverable: An artifact (diagram, table, list, schedule, etc.) that is generated by the activities of the methodology and is retained in the final requirements package.

delivery process: A set of activities completed by IT professionals to design and build information systems.

development life cycle: The three phases of a system as it proceeds from the beginning to the end of development—determine what is required, design a physical solution, and build and implement the solution.

DFD: *See* **Data Flow Diagram**.

DFD process: The representation of an activity of the system that transforms input data into output data.

diagram symbols: *See* Appendix B.

distributed system architecture: A system configuration in which both process and data may be located on multiple physical processors in multiple physical locations.

EI (External Inputs): Data that comes from an external agent and crosses the system boundary from outside to inside.

EIF (External Interface File): A group of logically related data that resides outside the boundaries of the proposed system and is maintained by another application. It is used by the proposed system for reference purposes only.

entity: An object about which data must be stored.

entity key: An attribute or group of attributes that uniquely identifies an instance of a data entity.

Entity Life Cycle Diagram (ELCD): A diagram that documents the states that an entity can hold and the events that cause a transition from one state to another.

Entity Process View (EPV): A model that includes an event diagram and the data model fragment required by the event response.

Entity Relationship Diagram (ERD): A data model that represents system data to be stored over time.

EO (External Output): Data that is generated by the system and crosses the system boundary from inside to outside.

EQ (External Inquiry): Data that passes from an external agent into the system and results in data retrieval and generation of an EO. No internal files are updated.

essential system: The system represented by the complete set of true, conceptual requirements.

event: *See* **business event**.

Event Diagram: A single-process DFD that documents the required inputs and outputs of an event response.

event partition: That part of an information system that responds to a single business event.

event response: The set of actions performed by an information system whenever a specific business event occurs [McMenamin and Palmer, 1984].

external agent: Something outside the system boundary that sends data to or receives data from the system.

foreign key: A primary key of one entity that is stored in another entity to provide a link between instances of the two entities.

Fourth-Generation Language (4GL): A high-level language that accelerates development and typically contains graphical user interface capabilities.

FPA: *See* **Function Point Analysis**.

FPC (Function Point Count): The measure of the size of the proposed system based on five system components and adjusted by a factor derived from GSCs. It is based on the conceptual system requirements.

function assembly: Placement of the event-response process fragments in the appropriate class as methods and data.

Function Point Analysis (FPA): A code-independent method for software project estimating that measures the size of a proposed information system based on the conceptual requirements.

fundamental entity: A real-world data entity found naturally in the problem domain and one that has no dependencies on other entities.

GSC (General System Characteristic): One of a set of 14 system characteristics used for determining an adjustment factor to be applied to the initial FPC of the transaction components and data components of the proposed system.

GSDI (General System Degree of Influence): The total degree of influence of all 14 GSCs.

GUI (Graphical User Interface): Specialized software made up of graphic techniques such as windows to input and retrieve information.

IFPUG (International Function Point Users Group): An organization, based in Westerville, Ohio, whose charter is research in Function Point Analysis (FPA) and the publishing of a manual of FPC practices (www.ifpug.org).

ILF (Internal Logical File): A group of logically related data that resides within the boundary of the proposed system and is maintained by the proposed system.

incremental development: The division of a proposed system into partitions that can be combined into subprojects and designed and implemented following different schedules.

Information Engineering (IE): A data-centered, process-sensitive approach that is applied to the organization as a whole (or a significant part, such as a division), rather than on an ad hoc, project-by-project basis [Whitten and Bentley, 1998].

inheritance: The means by which methods and attributes defined in one object class are automatically made available to another, subordinate class.

iteration: A procedure in which repetition of a sequence of operations yields results successively closer to a desired result.

Joint Application Design (JAD): *See* **Joint Application Workshop**.

Joint Application Workshop (JAW): A facilitated group session in which users and information system developers collaborate in the design of a component of an information system. These sessions harness the power of group dynamics. (Synonyms: *JAD, joint session, joint design session*)

leveled DFD: A Data Flow Diagram composed of more than one integrated process that has been decomposed from a higher level single-process parent diagram. The data flows across system boundaries are the same for both diagrams.

life cycle: *See* **development life cycle**.

LOC: Lines-of-code metrics based on coding productivity rates derived from an organization's history of software development or from published standards.

logical system: A term used in some methodologies to mean conceptual or nonphysical.

method: A unit of processing for a specific object class to be performed in response to a message. (Synonyms: *operation, service*)

minispec: A process specification.

multiple occurrence associative key: A key formed (concatenated) from the primary keys of two associated entities and not unique in the problem context.

n-tier client server: A term used to represent a client-server architecture with three or more tiers, typically containing a minimum of a user-interface layer (client), an application layer in the middle, and a database layer (server).

nonobjective: A business function that will *not* be included in the requirements being defined for a specific information system.

normalization: *See* **data normalization**.

object collaboration: The sending of messages between object classes to invoke operations (methods) with the purpose of completing a specified task or activity required as part of a response to a business event.

object partition: That part of an information system that contains the data and processing for a single object class.

Online Transaction Processing (OLTP): Interactive (not batch) processing of business transactions.

paradigm: A pattern or way of doing something.

partition: One of the parts of a system defined by rules of a methodology such as those defining events or objects and that can be targeted for separate development and implementation.

pathological connection: Lateral interfaces between components of a system; communication between components of a system that does not travel up or down the control hierarchy.

polymorphism: In an object-oriented environment, the capability of a named procedure to complete processing differently for different object classes.

primary key: The attribute of an entity in a data model that uniquely identifies a specific occurrence of the entity.

process: A component of a DFD that represents the transformation of data.

process specification: A structured English (pseudocode) representation of the logic of a DFD process.

program stub: A module without significant logic that represents and acts in place of the module to be subsequently developed to meet system requirements for data transformation.

prototype: A limited-function, working model of a subset of system processing.

pseudocode: A form of structured English that does not conform to a specific software language.

RAAD (Rapid Architected Application Development): A RAD approach for the design and build phases of system development preceded by the thorough analysis and specification of conceptual system requirements.

RAD (Rapid Application Development): The merger of various structured techniques with prototyping techniques and joint application development techniques to accelerate systems development [Whitten and Bentley, 1998].

relationship: The association of one entity in a data model with another entity.

release: A subset of a whole system that has been targeted for implementation; a system can be implemented in multiple releases.

requirements: *See* **system requirement**.

requirements creep: Change that occurs to the initial application requirements as a project progresses through the life cycle.

RET (Record Element Type): A subgroup of data elements within a file. (Example: commercial or individual order data)

scalable: The capability to expand an information system to more powerful hardware platforms and to hundreds or even thousands of users.

scenario: A description of a series of activities or events that accomplish a specific task.

scope creep: Change that occurs in the initial application requirements as a project progresses through the life cycle. (Synonym: *requirements creep*)

SDLC (Structured Development Life Cycle): Originally a structured methodology for systems development that followed a waterfall approach.

single occurrence associative key: A key formed (concatenated) from the primary keys of two associated entities and unique in the problem context.

state: Any of various conditions characterized by definite attribute values in which an entity may exist.

structured English: A form of the English language used to describe the logic of proposed system processing; it departs from typical sentence structure by using only the words needed to convey the processing logic.

subtype entity: A data entity that stores unique attributes and inherits other common attributes from a supertype entity with which it has a relationship.

supertype entity: A data entity that stores common attributes and has a relationship with one or more subtypes that hold unique attributes.

system behavior: The way in which a system reacts in response to the event triggers.

system data: The data stored over time required to support the generation of system output.

system DFD: A Data Flow Diagram that represents the interaction between the highest-level components of the system under study.

system processing: The transformation of data for which the system is responsible.

system requirement: A function or capability that a system must have to provide needed business support for the users of the proposed system.

System Response Table (SRT): A tabular representation of an information system's responses to business events.

time box: The relatively rigid time period or amount of time planned for an activity.

toolbox of techniques and methods: The methods and techniques that are used as needed as the analyst bounces back and forth among the ones that bring the most value to the project. Although the methods have some required order, they are used *iteratively* and in parallel and some may not be used at all. No order of use is implied.

trigger: A data flow that occurs in response to a business event and flows into the system, invoking the planned event response.

UAT: *See* **user acceptance testing**.

UFPC (Unadjusted Function Point Count): The measure of complexity of EI, EO, EQ, ILF, and EIF components of the proposed system.

UML (Unified Modeling Language): A modeling language or modeling notation (not a method or methodology) provided by the Rational Software Corporation for the design and development of object-oriented computer-based systems.

use case: A behaviorally related sequence of steps (a scenario), both automated and manual, for the purpose of completing a single business task [Whitten and Bentley, 1998].

User Acceptance Testing (UAT): Testing performed by the user group that verifies the correctness of the match between the software product and the system requirements. (Synonym: *acceptance testing*)

VAF (Value Adjustment Factor): A measure of the complexity of the 14 IFPUG GSCs.

version: *See* **release**.

waterfall methodology: A methodology in which each step depends on the prior step, and once completed, is seldom revisited.

white box: A system object that is examined by considering its internal logic or content.

References

Allen, Paul, and Stuart Frost, "An Integrated Component-Based Process," *Object Magazine,* February 1998, p. 36.

August, Judy H., *Joint Application Design,* Englewood Cliffs, N.J.: Prentice Hall, 1991.

Bohl, Marilyn, "An Open Systems Approach to Application Partitioning," *A Dynasty Technologies Inc. White Paper,* 1995, p. 1.

Coad, Peter, and Edward Yourdon, *Object-Oriented Analysis,* Englewood Cliffs, N.J.: Prentice Hall, 1990.

Davis, Alan M., *Software Requirements: Objects, Functions, and States,* Englewood Cliffs, N.J.: Prentice Hall, 1993.

DeMarco, Tom, *Structured Analysis and System Specification,* Englewood Cliffs, N.J.: Prentice Hall, 1979.

DeSmedt, William, "The Wolf at the Door," *Database Programming & Design,* April 1994, p. 64.

Function Point Counting Practices Manual, Release 4.0, Westerville, Ohio: International Function Point Users Group, 1994.

Function Point Counting Practices Manual, Release 4.1, Westerville, Ohio: International Function Point Users Group, 1999.

"IT Metrics For Success," *Information Week Online,* April 1999, p 2.

Jones, T. Capers, *Estimating Software Costs,* New York: McGraw-Hill, 1998.

————, *Conflict and Litigation between Software Clients and Developers,* Version 6, Burlington, Mass: Software Productivity Research, Inc., March 29, 1999.

King, David, *Project Management Made Simple,* Englewood Cliffs, N.J.: Prentice Hall, 1992.

Lewis, Mark, "Getting the Requirements," *Object Magazine,* November 1996, p. 44.

McMenamin, Stephen, and John Palmer, *Essential Systems Analysis,* Englewood Cliffs, N.J.: Prentice Hall, 1984.

Merriam-Webster's Collegiate Dictionary, Tenth Edition, Springfield, Mass: Merriam-Webster, Inc., 1995.

Rumbaugh, James, Michael Blaha, William Premerlani, Frederick Eddy, and William Lorensen, *Object-Oriented Modeling and Design,* Englewood Cliffs, N.J.: Prentice Hall, 1991.

Sanders, G. Lawrence, *Data Modeling,* Danvers, Mass: boyd & fraser, 1995.

Standish Group International, Inc., CHAOS report, available online: http://www.standishgroup/chaos.html, 1995.

Taylor, David, *Object Technology: A Manager's Guide,* Second Edition, Reading, Mass: Addison-Wesley, 1998.

Trustman, John, and Susan Meshako, "Dirty Little Secrets," *Intelligent Enterprise,* May 11, 1999, p. 16.

Weinberg, Gerald, *An Introduction to General Systems Thinking,* New York: John Wiley & Sons, 1975.

Whitten, Jeffrey, and Lonnie Bentley, *Systems Analysis and Design Methods,* Fourth Edition, Boston: Irwin/McGraw-Hill, 1998.

Wiley, Bill, research conducted at Taylor University, Upland, Ind., 1995–1999.

Yourdon, Inc., *Yourdon Systems Method,* Englewood Cliffs, N.J.: Yourdon Press, 1993.

Index

Addison-Wesley Computer and Engineering Publishing Group

How to Interact with Us

1. Visit our Web site

http://www.awl.com/cseng

When you think you've read enough, there's always more content for you at Addison-Wesley's web site. Our web site contains a directory of complete product information including:

- Chapters
- Exclusive author interviews
- Links to authors' pages
- Tables of contents
- Source code

You can also discover what tradeshows and conferences Addison-Wesley will be attending, read what others are saying about our titles, and find out where and when you can meet our authors and have them sign your book.

2. Subscribe to Our Email Mailing Lists

Subscribe to our electronic mailing lists and be the first to know when new books are publishing. Here's how it works: Sign up for our electronic mailing at **http://www.awl.com/cseng/mailinglists.html**. Just select the subject areas that interest you and you will receive notification via email when we publish a book in that area.

3. Contact Us via Email

cepubprof@awl.com

Ask general questions about our books.
Sign up for our electronic mailing lists.
Submit corrections for our web site.

bexpress@awl.com

Request an Addison-Wesley catalog.
Get answers to questions regarding your order or our products.

innovations@awl.com

Request a current Innovations Newsletter.

webmaster@awl.com

Send comments about our web site.

cepubeditors@awl.com

Submit a book proposal.
Send errata for an Addison-Wesley book.

cepubpublicity@awl.com

Request a review copy for a member of the media interested in reviewing new Addison-Wesley titles.

We encourage you to patronize the many fine retailers who stock Addison-Wesley titles. Visit our online directory to find stores near you or visit our online store: **http://store.awl.com/** or call **800-824-7799**.

Addison Wesley Longman
Computer and Engineering Publishing Group
One Jacob Way, Reading, Massachusetts 01867 USA
TEL 781-944-3700 • FAX 781-942-3076